THE AMERICAN PHILOSOPHER

GIOVANNA BORRADORI

THE AMERICAN PHILOSOPHER

Conversations with Quine,
Davidson, Putnam, Nozick, Danto,
Rorty, Cavell, MacIntyre,
and Kuhn

Translated by Rosanna Crocitto

The University of Chicago Press
Chicago and London

Giovanna Borradori has taught philosophy at Milan Polytechnic and Vassar College. She is the editor of *Recoding Metaphysics: The New Italian Philosophy*, and the author of *Il Pensiero Post-Filosòfico*. Currently she lives in New York City.

The University of Chicago Press, Chicago 60637
The University of Chicago Press, Ltd., London
© 1994 by The University of Chicago
All rights reserved. Published 1994
Printed in the United States of America
03 02 01 00 99 98 97 96 95 94   5 4 3 2 1

ISBN (cloth): 0-226-06647-9
ISBN (paper): 0-226-06648-7

Originally published as *Conversazioni americane con W. O. Quine, D. Davidson, H. Putnam, R. Nozick, A. C. Danto, R. Rorty, S. Cavell, A. MacIntyre, Th. S. Kuhn,* © 1991, Gius. Laterza & Figli.

Library of Congress Cataloging-in-Publication Data

Borradori, Giovanna.
    [Conversazioni americane. English]
    The American philosopher : conversations with Quine, Davidson, Putnam, Nozick, Danto, Rorty, Cavell, MacIntyre, and Kuhn / Giovanna Borradori ; translated by Rosanna Crocitto.
        p.   cm.
    Includes index.
    ISBN 0-226-06647-9. — ISBN 0-226-06648-7 (pbk.)
    1. Philosophy, American—20th century. 2. Philosophers—United States—Interviews. I. Title.
    B935.B6613   1994
    191—dc20   93-5294
                                                                     CIP

To Arturo

CONTENTS

PREFACE TO THE
ENGLISH EDITION

There are many distinctly European elements to this book: the very format of the literary conversation; its belief in the existence of a person-philosopher behind every theory; the recurrence of concepts such as the origin of ideas, the migration of intellectual trends, and their cross-fertilization; and, finally, the reasons for the selection, from the labyrinthine American scene, of these specific nine dialogues.

When I was confronted with the prospect of an English translation, I asked myself whether these conversations were not rather foreign to American cultural sensibility. But going again over the pages of Ralph Waldo Emerson reassured me that the attempt to explore the identity of the American scholar (or philosopher), though rare, is not foreign, and is certainly still worthwhile.

In addition to renewing my gratitude to the nine philosophers included in the volume, I wish to thank Jennifer Church for her comments and precious friendship, Michael Murray for believing so generously in my work, and all of my former colleagues at Vassar College for providing me with a warm and stimulating environment. I am particularly grateful to Rosette T. Uniacke, also from Vassar, for her dedicated help with the tapes. Finally, I would like to express my debt to T. David Brent, of the University of Chicago Press, for his patience and determination in converting this project from an idea into a reality.

New York, September 1993

PREFACE

When I began my journey through the world of American philosophy, I did not suspect that my *cahiers de voyage* would become the basis of this book. I thought that those pages and pages of notes and memoranda, along with the kilometers of recorded tape, would only be used to confront some judgments on the history of nineteenth-century American thought, the subject of a book I am currently writing for Editori Laterza. However, the intensity and the unexpected interrelation of these dialogues with nine of the most significant American philosophers persuaded me to give them an autonomous form.

The snowy morning spent with Willard Van Orman Quine and his "navigated" wisdom, the utopian impulse of Robert Nozick, the encyclopedic conversations with Hilary Putnam and Stanley Cavell—in the setting of Emerson Hall, in the heart of Harvard—were unforgettable moments. So, too, was the long walk with Richard Rorty, under the white portico of the University of Virginia, a miracle of Jeffersonian order; the discovery of the precise and remote world of Alasdair MacIntyre; the true New York evenings with Arthur C. Danto, often in the company of his wife Barbara; the discussions in the Boston townhouse of Thomas S. Kuhn; and, finally, the wanderings with Donald Davidson through the medieval setting of San Marino, where we were guests of Umberto Eco and his International Center of Semiotic and Cognitive Science.

I extend my gratitude to all of them. I would also like to thank

Aldo Giorgio Gargani, for his constant and affectionate encouragement; Enrico Mistretta for his enthusiasm in my projects; and the Fondazione di San Paolo di Torino, whose fellowship allowed me to finish the book.

New York, September 1990

The Atlantic Wall

A New Cartography

Only a few decades separate the Italian travels of Winckelmann, Goethe, and the masters of classicism from the transatlantic adventure of Alexis de Tocqueville, author of *Democracy in America*, the first manifesto on the American myth. Nevertheless, there is a fundamental difference between them. The first were *grands tours* on acting the story of origins, in search of the buried, yet vibrant, matrix of Western culture. Tocqueville's was a sort of *detour*, a courageous digression from the center to the periphery, reaching "the extreme confines of European civilization." America, the continent-nation of the mobile frontier, always presents itself to the European traveler as the edge of an unknown where the lines of a new history are being rearranged.

The novelty of this history also permeates contemporary American philosophical culture, which has been too often assimilated into the European pattern of events, and has rarely been the object of systematic analysis on its own terms. From a critical point of view, we Europeans lack the categories necessary for a coherent interpretation of American philosophy. As in a cubist painting, the contours appear dismembered, torn apart by an explosion that allows no return. Thousands of perspectives overlap simultaneously, each one suggested by a single, specialized point of view. To recompose the profile of this disjointed portrait is to challenge "the Atlantic wall," the screen of mutual misunderstanding that for years has divided the philosophical scenes on the two shores of the ocean.

The object of this book, which contains nine dialogues with some of the most emblematic protagonists of contemporary American philosophy, is to move through a wall that, unlike many others of past and present Europe, is made of water. To transcend the "wall of the Atlantic" does not mean to knock it down with a pickax, but to chart its currents, to navigate it, and to inhabit it.

For this purpose I have gathered here contributions from diverse places, with the hope of setting in motion a conversation among disciplinary areas that often do not communicate well with one another. The distinct logico-linguistic orientations of Willard Van Orman Quine and Donald Davidson are confronted with more dis- cursive and interdisciplinary trends of thought, such as Richard Rorty's and Hilary Putnam's versions of neo-pragmatism, and Stan- ley Cavell's neo-skepticism. The theory of pluralist anarchism for- mulated by Robert Nozick, in both the political and theoretical fields, is brought face to face with the neo-foundationalism of Arthur C. Danto, who is suspended in a disenchanted equilibrium between philosophical discourse and artistic experimentation. Thomas Kuhn's hypothesis on the alternating paradigms of scientific eras is measured against one of the most significant versions of the now widespread neo-historicist sensibility: Alasdair MacIntyre's ethics of "virtues."

The invitation to complete the "crossing" comes from these same protagonists on the American scene, and from the originality of their message, democratizing thought, exploring the subtle confines that separate the possibility of theory from the spector of totaliza- tion. In this philosophy there is no system, only an openness to new possibilities and the challenge of their integration. Like Tocqueville's journey, this one interrogates the boundaries of the known: the ever-mobile frontier becomes a theoretical category in itself, a new center, and is no longer the periphery of Western culture.

In the course of this itinerary, I attempted a new cartography of American philosophical culture. On the one hand, I have redesigned a more organic outline of the history of American philosophy after the Second World War. On the other hand, I have tried to include a still greatly misunderstood philosophical trend of thought that a segment of the American scene shares with European debates: this has to do with a propensity to elaborate on the epistemological value of one's own relationship to tradition. For many American authors, the dialogue with their most recent tradition, which is that of analytic philosophy, provides an essential means of intellectual progress. The understanding of this trend helps to promote what I believe is a new channel of communication between the two shores of the Atlantic. It is a mainly unexplored channel that narrows the distance between contemporary American philosophy, with its distinctly scientific self-representation, and the more literary European debates, extending from French post-structuralism to the many Italian versions of "weak thought" and postmodern hermeneutics.[1]

For the French, the point of departure remains structuralism, interwoven from the beginning with the Heideggerian problematic of ontological difference. For Italians the point of departure is a line of reflection which, starting with Heidegger and Nietzsche, permeates an entire sector of twentieth-century *mitteleuropean* philosophy. Instead, the tradition to which American thought constantly refers is that of analytic philosophy. This relation suggests that we describe its profile with the composite term "post analytic philosophy."[2]

1. For the concept of "weak thought" see Gianni Vattimo, *The End of Modernity* (1988); idem, *The Adventures of Difference* (1993); and the forthcoming anthology, *Weak Thought*, ed. Gianni Vattimo and Pier Aldo Rovatti, all published by Johns Hopkins University Press. As an introduction to the Italian debate, see issues 1 (1986) and 2 (1988) of the journal *Differentia*, especially Peter Carravetta's article, "Repositioning Interpretive Discourse: From the 'Crisis of Reason' to 'Weak Thought' " (*Differentia* 2:83–126).

2. This notion was advanced for the first time in the eponymous programmatic anthology *Post-Analytic Philosophy* (New York: Columbia University Press, 1985), edited by John Rajchman and Cornel West. It stands out as one of the few efforts at historical-critical recomprehension of the theoretical panorama of the United States. Gathering together theses that range from the philosophy of politics (by Thomas Nagel, John Rawls, T. M. Scanlon, Sheldon S. Wolin) to the theory of language (Donald Davidson and Hilary Putnam), from the philosophy of science (Thomas S. Kuhn and Ian Hacking) to aesthetics (Arthur C. Danto, Harold Bloom, and Stanley Cavell), the anthology traces the profile of a new intellectual community, taking its cue from the reelaboration of the imposing heritage of analytic philosophy. Leaning toward the pragmatist renaissance sustained by Richard Rorty and Richard J. Bernstein, who are also included in the volume, Rajchman's incisive introduction specifies

This type of thinking, about which the protagonists of this book confront one another, has not yet finished its interpretation of an earlier philosophical reality that, over the space of twenty years, changed the face of American debates. From the thirties to the sixties, from the eve of the Second World War to the Vietnam War, American philosophy ceased to be a socially engaged interdisciplinary enterprise, becoming instead a highly specialized occupation.

The analytic movement seems to be responsible for this metamorphosis. Featuring precise formal problems and hostile to any form of historical-literary erudition, it always posed itself in open opposition to that European body of thought—referred to as "Continental"—that, arising after Hegel's idealist turn, produced phenomenology and existentialism and promoted the creation of disciplines with a highly philosophical content, such as psychoanalysis.

With the exception of the transition figure of Quine, post-analytic thought reads the preceding analytic tradition according to two interpretations. The first could be described as an introspective journey into the labyrinth of what it means to do "analysis," conducted on the basis of its own linguistic instruments. Among the authors included in this collection, Davidson, who is most directly tied to the logical tradition, belongs on this first trajectory; also the political philosopher, Nozick; and the polymath thinker, Danto, who has extended his areas of interest from aesthetics to the philosophy of history.

The second vision is inspired instead by the desire to go beyond the analytic horizon. Questioning the errors and sins of analysis, and trying to build a new language and a spectrum of new references, this second axis includes philosophers as well-rounded as Putnam, Rorty and Cavell; but it does not exclude thinkers who are more active in specialized fields, such as philosophy of science in Kuhn's case and ethics in MacIntyre's. With its radical separation from the confines of analytic philosophy, this quest pushes on beyond the Pillars of Hercules: to the margins of meaning, language, and philosophical truth, seen and criticized in its function as a

some "directions of American philosophy after analysis." Among these are the emergence of a new "public" engagedness in philosophy; a general tendency toward "de-disciplinization," understood not so much as "collaboration between specialized fields, as the attempt to create new ones" (p. xiii); and a renewed interest in historical perspective, completely removed from the scientific basis of the analytic genre.

master key to the individual disciplinary and humanistic vocabularies, both political and scientific.

In my effort to redesign this "new cartography" of contemporary American philosophy, I aimed at being as complete and realistic as I could. But the virtual absence of any previous attempts to make historical and genealogical sense of this field made me rely exclusively on my individual perception. The philosophers who animate these conversations are, I hope, highly emblematic of the various regions of current discussion. However, I am aware that many others were left out. Among them, I would like to mention Nelson Goodman, who, together with Quine, shares the distinction of having brought a new way of thinking philosophically to the United States; Saul Kripke and Jerry Fodor, for their radical reshaping of the philosophy of language; John Searle, who, in the line of Wittgenstein and Austin, creatively reinvented "ordinary language philosophy"; Noam Chomsky, as the initiator of generativism; and, finally, John Rawls, who reinscribed political thought in the new frame of neo-contractualism.[3]

The Analytic Fracture

The analytic "adventure," begun in the mid-thirties, gave rise to an epistemological fracture in the body of American philosophy, a clean break that divided its history into two parts.

Because of the Nazi racial and political persecutions, an entire sector of *mitteleuropean* philosophers emigrated to the United States around the time of the Second World War, and permanently estab-

---

3. This "political" wing of the post-analytic current merits separate treatment (see note 9 regarding the debate on liberalism). Here we should at least cite Thomas Nagel, Ronald Dworkin, T. M. Scanlon, Sheldon S. Wolin, Roberto Unger, and Michael Walzer. The absence of John Rawls from this collection of dialogues is in no way intended to deny his centrality in the post-analytic context. In *A Theory of Justice,* written in 1971, his neo-contractualist proposition announced the independence of the moral horizon from the linguistic and epistemological preoccupations of analytic inquiry and revolutionized the field of political philosophy (see "A Kantian Conception of Equality" [*The Cambridge Review,* February 1975, pp. 94–99]). This affirmation of the reciprocal autonomy of the horizons of research opened the door to a new dynamic in ethical debate, in the context of which one can also reread the writings of Nozick and MacIntyre, different as they are from each other.

lished themselves overseas. The term "analytic philosophy" defines an area of study, with a spectrum of logical and linguistic interests, that arose in the shadow of this wave of migration. It includes such authors as Rudolf Carnap, Hans Reichenbach, Carl Hempel, Otto Neurath, and Herbert Feigl. More particularly, it refers to a neo-positivist direction of research that arose after the ideas of the Vienna Circle thinkers were planted on American soil.

There is no doubt that American philosophy arrived at this historical rendezvous very disoriented, and more than ever before open to a transfusion of new ideas. The founders of the first kind of pragmatism, Charles Sanders Peirce and William James, had died more than thirty years before. Even the youngest teacher of its interdisciplinary and public activity, John Dewey, was growing old, along with Franklin D. Roosevelt and the New Deal, which he had largely supported, and even inspired. In the 1950s, on the pragmatist horizon, some figures emerged who were more active in the debate on the human sciences: for example, the behavioral psychologist B. F. Skinner and the functionalist sociologist Talcott Parsons, founder of the theory of social systems.

In this atmosphere of the decline of the great myths, there began to emerge, for the first time since the death of Peirce in 1914, an interest in logic, particularly in its foundational role for mathematics. Inaugurated in Germany at the end of the century by Gottlob Frege and the Russian-born mathematician George Cantor, the initiator of set theory, this tendency was ultimately sealed by Bertrand Russell and Alfred North Whitehead, in England, with their *Principia Mathematica*, composed between 1910 and 1913.

The diffusion of the *Principia*, as well as the gradual delineation of a logistical wing within pragmatism, epitomized by C. I. Lewis of Harvard, created the conditions for an exchange with that area of *mitteleuropean* thought—Austrian, Czech, and Polish—designated logical positivism or neo-positivism. The Vienna Circle was the principal European moment of uniting these movements. This is the name with which from 1922 onwards the Berlin-born philosopher Moritz Schlick baptized his seminars, born in the climate of discussions with Hans Reichenbach on the significance of Einstein's theory of relativity. A major contribution to the philosophical definition of the Circle was made by their debate on Ludwig Wittgenstein's *Tractatus Logico-Philosophicus* (1921), a fundamental work for all the neo-positivists who subsequently emigrated to the United States.

In 1932, at the peak of this cultural revolution, a very young American—Willard Van Orman Quine—disembarked in Vienna, ready to be taken under the wing of the great Austrian masters. Prepared to dedicate his life to mathematical logic, which he was convinced was the only philosophical perspective of any importance, Quine was fresh from a doctorate at Harvard University, where he had studied under the guidance of Lewis and Whitehead, who had moved there from England in 1924.

From the time of Quine's first trip to Europe, the history of the Vienna Circle became entwined with that of American philosophy. In 1936, after the murder of Moritz Schlick on the steps of the University of Vienna at the hands of a Nazi student, the last remaining exponents of logical positivism emigrated to the United States, relying on the universities of Harvard and Princeton, thanks to the help of Quine in the first case and the mathematician Alonzo Church in the second.

In America, the definition of analytic philosophy has always been posed in opposition to European thought. In fact, the opposition between "analytic" and "Continental" philosophy is one of the most important historical consequences of the flight of logical positivism to the United States. Repudiating the previous transcendentalist and pragmatist trajectory that engaged it deeply on the public and interdisciplinary front, American philosophy changed face after the Second World War. As for the anti-metaphysical will that had pushed the representatives of the Vienna Circle to define themselves as "scientists" rather than humanists, philosophical thought in America closed itself to Europe, and above all to the many currents of existential and hermeneutic derivation, which are often branded even today as obscurantist and nihilist.

But the same opposition to metaphysics, that would become the cue for disciplinary and geographic isolationism for the analytic movement, was lived differently in the original debates of the Vienna Circle. Metaphysics represented a heritage that the Italian futurists could have defined as *passatista,* that is, conservative, verbose and incapable of assimilating the philosophical impact of the scientific revolutions that were just beginning to emerge from the shadows: from Albert Einstein's theory of relativity to Werner

Heisenberg's indeterminacy principle. With the same violence with which the artistic avant garde had wanted to remake the parameters of visual and auditory perception, logical positivism nourished itself on the dream of tearing philosophy away from metaphysical approximations and rebuilding it on a strictly scientific basis.

In the conviction that the logical symbolism developed by Frege and by Russell and Whitehead's *Principia Mathematica* was the instrument for the construction of an ideal and logically perfect language, the authors of the Vienna Circle proposed to create a "universal language" of science. The formulation of this language of unified sciences was to have the primary philosophical role of avoiding the discontinuity between words and experience as well as all the ambiguities of the common language on which the discourse of modern metaphysics had been founded, ever since Hegel's idealist reaction against Kant.

The emblem of this dream was the project of the *International Encyclopedia of Unified Sciences,* completed at the end of the thirties by Carnap and Neurath with the collaboration of the Americans Charles Morris and John Dewey at the University of Chicago. Composed of a series of monographs, each dedicated in turn to a particular philosophical discipline, the *Encyclopedia* did not aim at constructing "the" system of science, so much as at integrating the methods and contents of each individual science.

As the years went by, the universal project of the neo-positivist discourse was gradually translated into a minute attention to logical detail. The Vienna Circle, in fact, had bequeathed to analytical philosophers in America the unshakable certainty that they were working in a field that was stable in time and possessed well-delineated disciplinary outlines. The result was a general propensity toward the work of attentive logical clarification rather than promoting new visions of the world.

These rigorous techniques of exposition and argumentation, with their stylistically aseptic writing that strove to be as objective as possible, brought to an end the public era of American philosophy. That era had been inaugurated in the middle of the nineteenth century by Ralph Waldo Emerson, poet, writer, preacher of the Unitarian church, teacher of the philosophical movement of transcendentalism, and it had reached its high point in the first decades of the twentieth century with the multi-sided pragmatism of John Dewey.

Post-analytical Recomposition

From the point of view of the sociology of knowledge, the fracture introduced by the analytical movement into the body of American philosophy had two concomitant outcomes: it isolated philosophy from interchange with the world of humanistic reflection, and it channeled a portion of philosophical interests in the direction of other disciplines. In fact, new areas of academic debate such as textual theory, cultural criticism, and gender studies,[4] which were born contemporaneously with the confinement of philosophy within the boundaries of logical analysis, became major American repositories of European thought. This is true especially for the most recent phase of European thought, which is epitomized in the context of the humanities in America, by the French post-Heideggerian scene and by German post-Marxism, in a cluster of authors that includes the philosophers of *différence,* among them Michel Foucault, Gilles Deleuze, and Jacques Derrida, and some heirs of the Frankfurt school, such as Jürgen Habermas.

The arrival of neo-positivism on the campuses of the East Coast on the eve of the Second World War has therefore left as its heritage two complementary phenomena. First, an irreversible professionalization of philosophy, which has become divorced from public debate and, more generally, from the emerging trends in intellectual history. Second, an increasing philosophical literacy in the humanities, which has allowed new, theoretically dense disciplines to flourish, though rendering the philosophical themes they treat more literary. The anti-humanistic closure of analytic philosophy has

4. This flourishing of new disciplines, which includes performance studies, the subdivisions of gender studies into gay and lesbian theory, women's studies, African-American studies, and many others, has united much of European ontological reflection under the heading of social alterity. A good example of this usage is the shading of the French philosophy of *différence,* traceable in its origin to the ontological problematic opened by Heidegger on the irreconcilability of Being and entity, toward the "differences" emerging from new social identities, starting with feminism and ethnic minorities.

meant that a great part of the dialogue with nonanalytic European thought has been maintained by literary scholars who have worked to create programs and centers of interdisciplinary research specifically for this purpose.[5]

If it is possible to specify a common trajectory for the new inscription of philosophical problematics—ontological, epistemological, metaphysical—in an aesthetic-literary context, it is certainly in the extension of the notion of "text."[6] The translation of European philosophy into a "textualist" vocabulary represents a reality on the contemporary American scene that only in the last few years has begun to be analyzed by the broader horizon of awareness opened by post-analytic thought. The publication of Richard Rorty's *Consequences of Pragmatism* in 1980 acted as a detonator. Today discussion of the real "wall" that has divided philosophy on the two shores of the Atlantic is a central theme of theoretical debate, as can be seen by its recurrence in the dialogues of this collection.

However, in tracing a new cartography of American thought, the philosophical density of some branches of the humanities makes for some confusion. This confusion increases rather than diminishes if one recognizes the decisively original character of some of the "textual" theories. This is certainly the case with the Yale Critics, Paul de Man, Geoffrey Hartman, and J. Hillis Miller. It is to them that we owe, since the 1960s, the original elaborations of deconstruction, inaugurated in France by Jacques Derrida.

---

5. Among many others are the Center for Twentieth-Century Studies at the University of Wisconsin, directed by Cathleen Woodward, and inspired by Ihab Hassan, a now-historic figure in the postmodern debate; the Center for the History of Consciousness at the University of California, Santa Cruz, headed by Hayden White, which is host to innumerable conferences on "textualism" and deconstruction; and the Center for the Critical Analysis of Contemporary Culture at Rutgers University, oriented more toward the human sciences and, above all, to exchange between philosophy and sociological thought.

6. In America, the concept of an autonomous and irreducible "text" acquired a new centrality with the popularization of the New Criticism at the beginning of Second World War. To deny referentiality and historical context to the text was to assign criticism a basis of "objectivity" independent of the author's intention. This denial of subjectivity in reading introduced into literary theory a range of philosophical issues similar and in part parallel to the ones advanced by structuralism in France. The spread of Continental philosophy into departments of English, comparative literature, and foreign languages and literatures, was therefore facilitated by an inter-

Alongside the Yale Critics, and also because his name has been associated with this group for a long time, emerges the figure of another literary critic, Harold Bloom, who has reread the ontological import of the discourses of Heidegger and Gadamer in light of the interpretative tradition of Hebrew mysticism. Finally, among others belonging to this constellation, there are Edward Said and Fredric Jameson, who, in different ways, have proposed applying the textual key to the social scene, translating the epistemological thematic of the "other" (something else, and abstract singular), into the sociological one of "others" (someone else, a specific plural), which is rendered all the more inscrutable because of the superimposition and intersection of ethnic minorities.

An interrogation of the residual significance of philosophy condenses around the notion of "text." Stripped of its role as queen of the sciences, philosophy reemerges clothed in the remnants of its former role, more democratic, more literary, more a matter of a writing among writings. As a transcultural voice that guarantees to posterity a great polyphonic chorus of knowledge, this new, highly theoretical version of humanism is reborn as post-philosophical thought.[7] The prefix post suggests an exploration of the margins of the same dissolution of the historical significance of philosophy.

It is interesting to contrast this process of philosophical appropriation by the humanities with the post-analytic framework that the interlocutors of these conversations take up for themselves. At the center of its reflections remain those transformations the analytic movement wrought upon the body of American thought: on the one hand becoming more and more indifferent to the main trends animating continental-European philosophy, and, on the other, cutting its links with philosophical thinking preceding the Second World War, especially with that parabola that stretches from the transcendentalism of Emerson to the many pragmatists of the nineteenth and twentieth centuries, such as Peirce, James, and Dewey.

---

est in the notion of the text. Around the end of the sixties, New Criticism was supplanted by deconstruction, which is, instead, of post-structuralist derivation.

7. This line of debate, which no longer allows any disciplinary segmentation, integrates textual theory and deconstruction into the aesthetic experimentations of postmodernism (see Richard Rorty, *Consequences of Pragmatism: Essays 1972–1980* [Minneapolis: Minnesota University Press, 1988]; and Giovanna Borradori, *Il pensiero post-filosofico* [Milan: Jaca Book, 1988]).

The refusal to place the work of philosophical argumentation within a historical perspective was a distinctive trait of the analytic current from its beginning in logical positivism. Starting with his discussion of the significance of relativity in *Philosophy of Space and Time* (1928), Hans Reichenbach envisioned philosophy as pure epistemology, entrusting it with the duty of discovering the basic principles of scientific knowledge through logical analysis. A conceptual instrument as objective as it is metahistorical, the level of analytical reflection tore philosophy out of the passage of time. It protected philosophy from the degradation that inevitably causes visions of the world to decay.

Only two years after Reichenbach's declarations, Moritz Schlick maintained in *The Transformation of Philosophy,* that rather than being a science understood as a collection of truths, philosophy was a series of acts that clarified the sense of propositions. In *The Logical Construction of the World,* Carnap then reduced the significance of philosophy to the purely logical analysis of scientific discourse. Logic and scientific syntax thus came to coincide in a present without history which, no more than twenty years later, some post-analytical authors, especially Kuhn and Rorty, would dare to question.

The Metamorphosis of Quine

Secluded within the walls of analysis, American philosophy was one of the few disciplines that remained almost indifferent to the great events of post-world-war history, from Korea to McCarthyism. Philosophy had to wait more than two decades for post-analytic research to question its isolation. The movement is led by authors who all experienced the Second World War at a young age, and were all deeply influenced by the great *mitteleuropean* émigrés during their student days and throughout the crucial years of their development, until they became teachers.

Quine is the exception, a figure who embodies these changes. He knew the group of neo-positivists in Europe, when they were still working together in the synergy of the Vienna Circle at the beginning of the 1930s. Quine arrived at the dawn of the Nazi era, from an America still enraptured by Dewey's humanistic charm and by the promise of the New Deal, and his visit to Vienna in 1932 is one of those unforeseeable events that change the course of the history of ideas.

It is from this moment onward that one can mark the beginning of analytic philosophy in America. Following the mass migration of the great European logicians and the proselytizing work of the young Quine and a few others, American philosophy had, by the second half of the 1930s, entered and made itself at home in the labyrinth of logical inquiry. But, as a true king of the labyrinth, Quine immediately demonstrated his double identity: he had the head of an analytical philosopher, equipped with the most sophisticated Viennese logic, implanted on the body of an American thinker, pragmatic and tied to the method of experimental verification.

Hence, is he the last of the analytic philosophers, or the first of the post-analytic? Even if the question remains a dilemma for many, it does not remain so in this context, in which Quine occupies the key role as the precursor of a whole generation In fact, it is Quine who brings on stage the first great act of post-analytic thought: a rereading of logical positivism on the basis of American demands for a pragmatist and behaviorist matrix.

After ten years dedicated to one of the most frequently recurring problematics of the Vienna Circle, the role of logic in the foundation of mathematics, culminating in the publication of *Mathematical Logic* in 1949, Quine returned from the war to deliver the first major post-analytical attack on logical positivism. The title of the 1951 essay "The Two Dogmas of Empiricism," which was born out of discussions with another forerunner of post-analytical thought, Nelson Goodman, symbolizes the content of the attack. It takes the form of a refutation of perhaps the most crucial subject in the Viennese discourse, the distinction between analytic and synthetic judgments, on which rested the epistemological primacy of logical analysis, and from which, significantly, the name of "analytic" philosophy was derived.

For logical positivism, at least in its first formulation, analytic propositions (for example, "if it rains then it rains"), insofar as they lack empirical content, are the only necessary conditions of knowledge. In contrast, the synthetic propositions ("in such place at such a time it rains") are *a posteriori* assertions, and their truth therefore depends, aside from linguistic factors, on the external reality to which they refer. Necessity is then attributed only to analytic truth which, without saying anything about reality, is founded on the syntactic-semantic properties of language.

Quine's criticism consists in demonstrating the impossibility of making a distinction between these two logical orders. Although he admits that it is possible to organize analytic judgments into coherent systems, such as logic and mathematics, he does not admit that they belong to a pure form of logic.

Unlike the neo-positivists, Quine maintains that an analytic affirmation such as "every bachelor is an unmarried man" does not correspond to a crystalline logical proposition (such as, "every x is an x"), since the truth of the latter proposition derives from the fact that x does not denote anything, while the truth of the former depends in great part on the significance of its constitutive terminology. Here, then, the notion of analyticity is translated into that of synonymy, upon which, however, it is not possible to erect the same pretensions to absolute necessity.

Quine would not have arrived at these conclusions without that distinctively American pragmatist tradition which is so important for the emergence of post-analytic philosophy. In the case of Quine, this is not a public and experimental pragmatism in the style of John Dewey (as it is, for example, for Rorty), but rather a post-Kantian heritage derived through the mediation of logic and epistemology by C. I. Lewis, from which it borrows some linguistic instruments indispensable to the great post-analytic turn.

Alongside this, Quine assimilates the moves of ontological and pluralistic reflection which, begun at the turn of the century by William James, continued in the ramifications of psychological thought through functionalism and behaviorism, to which Quine was explicitly linked through his close collaborative relationship with Skinner. The reconstruction of such an ontological horizon, which had been censored *a priori* by the authors of the Vienna Circle (at least until their American emigration), marks the boundaries of Quine's Copernican revolution.

I believe this leap toward Skinner to be crucial to that very issue that locates Quine at the center of post-analytic philosophy: the indeterminacy of translation. What type of difficulty would one encounter in translating the language of a completely unknown

culture or tribe? Against the backdrop of an anthropological scenario, analyzed through the experimental lens of behaviorism and
oriented toward a demonstration of logical order, Quine shows that,
paradoxically, it would be possible to draw up a series of "manuals
of translation" that were different from and incompatible with one
another. While remaining faithful to the individual expressive dispositions of the authors, each manual would carve out a finite universe of communication, without furnishing the instruments for a
universal translation.

From Kuhn's theory about the paradigms of scientific evolution,
to Rorty's assertion of the "mortality" of epistemological vocabularies, to MacIntyre's ethic of "virtues," the post-analytic universe still
has not finished discussing this nodal issue, which Quine first
showed in *Word and Object* (1960) and in the essay "Ontological
Relativity" (1969). It is a crucial issue, because it represents a point
of contact between American post-analytical thought and the postmodern *différends* enunciated by Jean-François Lyotard and French
post-structuralism.[8]

The Intersubjective Necessity of Knowledge

Like the mythical Dioscuri, Castor and Pollux, Davidson and Putnam are Quine's most direct descendants. Very different in their
elaboration of his heritage, they have both inched a little nearer
than their teacher to the edge of the post-analytic abyss. Davidson
tries to integrate the question of intersubjectivity into the coldly
perceptive scaffolding of empiricism, in which Quine still finds himself entangled. Putnam reproposes the theme of a pragmatist realism, extended not only to the epistemological, but also to the ethical
and moral realms.

Only ten years younger than Quine, Davidson has followed him
since the time of the Second World War, when they both volunteered as Naval officers. Compared to Quine, the first great demysti-
fier of the dogmas of empiricism, Davidson goes even further.

8. This link was one of the most frequently recurring subjects of debate at the
Franco-American colloquium *La traversée de l'Atlantique*, excerpts of which were
published in a monographical issue of "Critique," 456 (May 1985), edited by Vincent
Descombes. Specific references to this link are found in Lyotard's texts, *The Postmodern Condition* and *Driftworks*.

If it is indeed true that we acknowledge Quine as having saved the very possibility of the philosophy of language, pulling down the barriers between the architecture of thought (analytic propositions) and its content (synthetic propositions), it is also true that Quine does not question the legitimacy of the epistemological subject, which, for him as for the empiricists, is in some way "prior" to the world. This view is ultimately Cartesian, and even solipsistic, because it is prisoner to the conviction that to each of us is given the ability to construct our world, starting from original given perceptions.

According to Davidson, we have here to do with a sort of "third dogma" of empiricism, which we must dismantle by inserting into its center the ethical and linguistic question of intersubjectivity. Neither language nor the mind organizes perceptible reality according to fixed conceptual schemes, since they and the world are all part of an intersubjective conceptual matrix.

Thus, even Quine's thesis on the incompatibility of manuals of translation becomes questionable, once Davidson claims that it is not possible to lose the faculty of speaking a language while maintaining at the same time the capacity to think. To think is to communicate. The entire universe, subjective and objective, is trapped in a hermeneutic mesh of signs. Reality itself is nothing other than a coagulation of language and interpretation.

Neurology—the physical reality of nervous stimulation caught, by dint of its unrepeatability, in its own private perceptiveness— does not lie at the origin for Davidson, as it does for Quine. What Davidson conveys to post-analytic thought is that the subject retains no "privacy of the mind," no possibility of analyzing perceptions or reactions in a strictly subjective sense, but only "events" that depend on the subject being in permanent exchange with other human beings: with others, speaking and communicating, interacting with them in the same context of meanings.

The voyage of thought and of knowledge has neither matrix nor root, subjective or objective. It can never be brought back to a beginning; it can only be ascribed to the dynamic of a triangular effort that implies at least two interlocutors and a context of shared situations.

Putnam articulates the theme of the necessary intersubjectivity of knowledge differently than Davidson. In tune with many other post-analytic thinkers, from Rorty to MacIntyre, he picks up the interrupted thread of ethical foundationalism typical of the pragmatists, among whom the figure of William James is dominant.

In opposition to Davidson, Putnam claims that a realm of objectivity still exists: the moral one of *beliefs*. The sphere of such beliefs must be allowed to be the basis of a new realism, even if it is only contextual, applicable to a specific period and to a specific situation. To deny the existence of the multiplicity of conceptual schemes, dissolving them into a single interactive scheme, as Davidson does, is to run the risk of definitively losing the referent, and with it constructivity, the incisive weapon of philosophical discourse. It is for this reason that the possibility of a "contextual" foundation of the world must not be abandoned, even if, after the pragmatists, it cannot be understood in other than moral terms.

Against the formalism grafted by the Viennese onto the trunk of American tradition, and in tune with the postulates of pragmatism, Putnam revitalizes the thrust of realist thought. It is not necessary to reach a more ultimate foundation than that of *beliefs*: in their organic unity, they form a recurring "moral image of the world," a sort of canon of moral objectivity that even in its contextual relativity proposes itself as *the* reality.

Philosophy, according to Putnam, is not a method of abstract epistemological control, such as the analytical tradition understands it to be. There is no universal method that permits the settlement of a disagreement between two interlocutors independently of the content of the discussion. Instead, what is at play is the moral reality of a thought, understood as a synthesis of beliefs around its form and its contents. What interests this neo-realist *après la lettre,* and what marks him specifically within the post-analytic group, is not his affirmation of pluralism against monism, so much as his taking for granted a multiplicity of worlds and the exploration of their value as "moral objectivity."

Putnam's realist proposal therefore contributes to post-analytic thought the hypothesis of a moral foundation for knowledge. Contrary to analytic philosophy, he puts into play again a humanistic synergy between the disciplines. But the recognition of moral priority is the heritage of a series of libertarian experiences that led some post-analytic thinkers into the role of "engaged" philosophers, especially during the sixties.

In the case of Putnam, this engagement assumed in an early period the form of a real militancy in the ranks of the American left
and in the pacifist movement against the war in Vietnam. In a later
period, it transformed itself into an interest in Judaism, understood
in a way that offered a mystical and salvational reading with respect
to the meaning of philosophy.

The Challenge to Conceptual Formalism

Criticism of the normative value of the analytic approach is typical
not only of Hilary Putnam; it forms an element of continuity among
all post-analytic thinkers. In the philosophies of Robert Nozick and
Arthur C. Danto it assumes configurations that are in some ways
complementary: in the case of Nozick, it is a matter of radical dis-
sent from the coercive impetus implicit in the formalism of the
analytic turn of mind. That same transparency in philosophical argumentation, where the analytic movement located the confines
within which thought could be legitimate, coincides for Nozick with
a repressive epistemological model against which it is indispensable
to pose an alternative. According to Danto, however, criticism translates itself into an aestheticization of its formalist impetus. The
analytic conceptual horizon survives, though weakened, in his fascination with the architectonic element of thought and the values of
harmony and beauty that it implies.

Nozick's libertarian alternative starts from a critical elaboration
of the notion of *argument,* which, after having traversed the entire
history of Western philosophy, becomes deified first by the logistical
intensity of the Vienna Circle, and then by the analytic movement.
The repressive potential of argument is already implicit in its literal
meaning in English, that is, "violent dispute."

Along with Putnam and many other post-analytic thinkers,
among them Cavell and MacIntyre, Nozick will not admit that philosophy can be reduced to a pure science of argumentation. He does
not want to accept that given fixed premises and a proof he would
necessarily derive one, and only one, conclusion from them, because
it is precisely this scheme that led the analytic movement to think
of the truth as victory over the interlocutor. Rather than force somebody to believe by constructing an incontrovertible argument, it

is more morally legitimate and more epistemologically creative to stimulate the interlocutor to alternative ways of thinking.

The notion of *explanation* can be skillfully extracted from the analytic vocabulary and reinscribed onto a new map of values and objectives. Posing itself in contrast to the coercive impetus of argument, this notion represents Nozick's principal contribution to the post-analytic turn. The objective of knowledge cannot be reached through the presentation of an infallible proof so much as in the moral improvement of the individual, pushed to deepen his or her own vision of the world and to communicate more freely with others.

Nozick's theoretical work has been nourished by the dream of tearing philosophy from the primitive and agonistic spirit of dispute and of reestablishing it on a new, more pluralistic basis of understanding. Since *Anarchy, State, and Utopia* (1974), this dream has been reflected in the field of political philosophy in the form of an anarchist and democratic utopia.

In contrast to Nozick's emancipatory position, oriented toward liberating philosophy from the overly rigid armor of analytical formalism, stands the neoclassical figure of Danto, who tries to redeem the universe of logical analysis through the categories of beauty, measure, and harmony.

For this philosopher, raised in close contact with the experimental, artistic avant garde at the end of the Second World War, the instruments of analysis are the only ones that give reason to the "equilibrium" that unfailingly describes every coherent conceptual structure. This is an equilibrium whose mystery is captured in the capacity to connect ideas according to the physiological perfection of the organism. Logical analysis reaches its goal and demonstrates its transcendental and foundational value by retracing mental and material objects back to their constituent parts.

The average American canonization of analytical discourse is an academic rigidification that Danto, in accord with the whole post-analytic movement, criticizes and would like to go beyond. But, unlike Nozick and Putnam, he does not express a systematic opposition to it. Analysis, for Danto, is the purest style of thought, crystalline and "according to nature," for a philosophy whose objective, analogous to that of art, is to reconstruct a Hegelian "sensible materialization" of ideas.

Irony and Dismay: Two Styles of Secularization

Putting analysis in the position of one style of reasoning among other possible styles pulls the teeth of its epistemology. This position, which Danto welcomes as if it were a poetic, takes on an explosive critical force in the work of a series of other post-analytic authors. Two thinkers who differ greatly in their language and conclusions, Richard Rorty and Stanley Cavell, share the idea that the analytic adventure is a style of thought that has covered over a clearly delimited historical gap in the development of Anglo-American philosophy.

If it is true that, starting with Quine and continuing with Davidson, Nozick, and Danto, the analytic project has been hollowed out from the inside using its own tools, with Rorty and Cavell it finds itself attacked from the outside. Cut off from its ties with the present, it is embalmed as a museum piece, its scientific hypotheses seen as one system among many when rechanneled into a historicist world view.

The analytical movement is accused of a tangle of faults, such as canonizing a philosophical discourse that remains within rigid disciplinary and professional confines, bleakly isolating philosophy from history, culture, and society. This knot was created by the analytical isolation, but it is untied with the recovery of two crucial traditions of thought in the intellectual history of the United States, pragmatism and transcendentalism.

Rorty was the first to resurrect in a new key that distinctively American line of thought inaugurated at the end of the nineteenth century by Charles Sanders Peirce and William James. Thanks to the long life of John Dewey, that tradition grew throughout the first half of the twentieth century, only to disappear, swallowed up by the Viennese immigration between the two world wars. Cavell, on the other hand, insists on transcendentalism: that first American philosophical movement that rose on a wave of suggestions from European idealism and reached its apex towards the middle of the nineteenth century with Ralph Waldo Emerson and Henry David Thoreau.

In Rorty's neo-pragmatist hypothesis, Dewey offers a pattern that has not been improved on but is hardly exhaustive. Alongside the master of American pragmatism, Rorty expands the post-analytic horizon by revaluating the line of Continental thinkers that leads through Nietzsche, Freud, and Heidegger, who had been judged obscure and nihilistic by the deities of neo-positivism.

The nucleus of Rorty's own neo-pragmatism is found in the convergence that he recognizes between pragmatism and the various criticisms of metaphysical absolutism developed along this line of European thought. He proposes a completely secularized philosophy. Stripped of any absolute epistemological role, the queen of the sciences takes on a more flexible, "democratic" form that is more open to stimulation from other disciplines.

Thus, philosophy is no longer thinkable in the Kantian terms of a "tribunal of pure reason." Rather, it opens a new field for informed and engaged dilettantism, whose agents will not be professionals of argumentation, but polypragmatic thinkers in the Socratic tradition, intent upon renewing the themes and dynamics of that Great Conversation which is culture.

Freed from the constraints of analysis, which wanted it to be a decisively scientific subject, philosophy has understood that there is no finite number of questions to be answered or a finite number of fundamental issues. Repeating a leitmotiv universally shared by the post-analytic thinkers, Rorty suggests that, in this new phase, the values of foundation and system are replaced by the values of proliferation and plurality. These provide a lens through which philosophy can appear in a new dimension: "post-philosophical culture."

Even epistemology gets defined in terms of style, as one kind of writing among others, whose access to truth is not superior to any other narrative genre. The choice of the epistemological "style" derives from the efficiency of its interpretative tools, which have been tested through centuries of Western history. Allergic to any form of foundationalism, either analytical or phenomenological, this new post-philosophical culture abandons itself to the dream of a new humanistic solidarity, one that is shared by nations, by people, and by the various disciplines all on the basis of the mortality and the contingency of their respective vocabularies.

The Voltairean irony that characterizes Rorty's shrewd pragmatism is counterbalanced by the neo-romantic impetus of Stanley Cavell. For him, the embodiment of the ideal engaged, polymath intellectual of the new post-analytic trend is not Dewey but a character far removed from the European emigration between the two wars: Ralph Waldo Emerson, the preacher, poet, and philosopher of Puritan Massachusetts, who was caught between the dialectical echoes of German idealism and the meditative ecstasies of Buddhism. However, like Rorty, Cavell does not depict America as an isolated continent; alongside Emerson, he lets other stars shine and articulate the luminosity of the constellation he proposes. Cavell, alone among the post-analytic authors, re-proposes consideration of the skeptical tradition in an original and unexpected fashion. From his perspective, skepticism is not seen as a realm of the disenchanted; it does not take on the characteristic indifference toward universal projects of knowledge that form its standard image from Pyrrho and Carneades to Montaigne and Hume.

For Cavell, on the contrary, skeptical thought brings to light the drama of self-awareness, embraced in its romantic meaning as a disparity between the finite and the infinite, a despair born of the confrontation between human finitude and the many mysteries of earthly existence: life, death, the universe.

Mediating between romantic reminiscences rooted in old Europe and transcendental echoes with decidedly American roots, Cavell's renewed attention to the problem of subjectivity makes his most specific contribution to the post-analytic movement. He locates this problematic, for the twentieth century, between the lines of philosophers such as John Austin and Ludwig Wittgenstein. Thick with existential excavations, the pages of this master of *ordinary language* illuminate a sensibility to the finite dimension of the quotidian that enters into a prodigious alchemy with the intuitions about the moral value of subjectivity advanced by skepticism.

The Historical Obsolescence of Vocabularies

By announcing his thesis on the indeterminacy of translation, Quine brought into the post-analytical world the idea of the untranslatability of individual vocabularies—historical, cultural, philosophical— into a universal lingua franca. Like a deep vibration, this conviction clearly animates Rorty's pluralistic epistemology, in which philosophy retains the duty of mediating meanings in a way that permits the individual vocabularies to comprehend one another, without any longer providing the key for translating them into a neutral and transparent language.

More than that, this thesis also appears to be central in the context of two other post-analytic visions, that of Alasdair MacIntyre, who denies that ethics can aspire to absolutely transparent principles beyond the historical context from which it draws its inspiration; and that of Thomas S. Kuhn, the first American philosopher to tear science away from the ancient rationalistic dream, organizing its development instead into a series of "scientific" visions of the world, or discontinuous paradigms in perennial fluctuation.

Moving with a new agility between the meshes of historicism, and in particular those woven by his Mediterranean predecessor, Giambattista Vico, MacIntyre's first step is to assign the liberal project to its ideological context. The liberal project is one of the most frequently recurring points of reference in the post-analytic universe of discourse.[9] In MacIntyre's view, liberalism is such a basic nutrient in the diet of every Anglo-American philosopher that it appears indispensable to intellectual life. On the contrary, he insists, its destructive nature must be revealed, based as it is on the progressive impoverishment of the traditional form of "community" and on the consequent dissolution of those human and social ties that since the time of ancient Greece have been the irreplaceable ingredient in our cultural progress.

Like natural languages, intellectual and moral worlds cannot be

---

9. In the plethora of theories, currents, and individual positions which figure in post-analytic thought, liberalism is still a crucial problematic. Rorty reproposes it in an epistemological key, as a requisite of solidarity among the disciplines; Rawls's theory of justice gives it a neo-contracturalist twist in which the egalitarian principle is based on a mental experiment, or at least stipulated by individual entities from behind "a veil of ignorance"; Sandel opposes himself to Rawls, maintaining that no contractualist choice can be made in the abstract about precise contents; Nagel, in turn, eliminates the model of antagonistic social interests and suggests the simple coexistence of diverse "modes" of the egalitarian principle. These positions of general reevaluation are joined by more critical readings of liberalism. Among its critics are Scanlon, who is inclined to a historical recontextualization of contractualism; Wolin, who attempts the redefinition of a project of Jacobin revolutionary action as a premise for the global transformation of society; and, finally, Roberto Unger who, mediating between Habermas's theory of communicative action and Rawls's new contractualism, is committed to launching a new version of "emancipatory social experimentalism."

translated from one into another. There is no canonical language in which to measure, confront, and judge the values, the reasons, the virtues expressed by a specific cultural universe. After the failure of the Enlightenment project, of which liberalism is, according to MacIntyre, an unfortunate epigone, the twentieth century has found itself in the most radical ethical despair, which has left as the only open alternative Nietzsche's nihilist overcoming of all principles and all morality.

Today, having reached the "heart of darkness" of the modern era, it is precisely this awareness of the destructiveness of Enlightenment reason, the parent not only of liberalism but also of the universalism of analytic philosophy, that makes us hope for a new renaissance. Classical Greece, an old love of MacIntyre since his debut as a classicist, provides the harmonious scenery, while the Aristotelian theory of "virtue" gives it a framework. The totalizing and universal image of virtue disappears, multiplying itself into a constellation of values more contextualized within the real histories of specific human communities.

In tune with the ethical reflections of MacIntyre, Kuhn also announces the death of the rationalistic vision of the progress of science. His vision is Sagittarius, the archer, half animal and half man, who tried to exorcise his ties with this earth, firing his arrows of knowledge far into space, as if to conquer the entire universe. Science, according to Kuhn, is quite different from this. Its progression is historical, and its results ineluctably mortal.

Scientific advancement, says Kuhn, is characterized by two phases: that of "normal science" and that of "revolutionary breaks." The first consists in gradually imposing a theoretical system, a sort of world view combining ideals and techniques of experimentation, theory, and method, that Kuhn defines as a "paradigm." The Ptolemaic and Galilean systems are examples of scientific paradigms that have their legitimation constantly confirmed by the community of researchers who work at their articulation. But, like a meteorite that cuts a path and breaks the archer's arrow, the transition phase intervenes at a certain point in the life of the paradigm. There comes a period of crisis in which its scientific and philosophical presuppositions undergo reevaluation—a period in which, slowly and progressively, the consensus of the scientific community crumbles and scientific language transforms itself.

In tune with Rorty and MacIntyre, Kuhn maintains that science, like philosophy, culture, and ethics, is constituted by a succession, often a coexistence, of different paradigms, perspectives, and mental frameworks, all absolutely independent of one another and mostly untranslatable. The career of science no longer aims at attaining ever-larger portions of the truth; it is defined by a simple evolutionary energy. This affirmation aims at the heart of Viennese philosophy, the idea that science and philosophy (understood as scientific undertakings) can always and in all conditions rely on the existence of "observative protocols" that are protected from time and from the obsolescence of languages. Instead, Kuhn issues a warning to post-analytic philosophy: during the phase of revolutionary rupture, the scientist is alone, and he cannot hope for any vocabulary in support or confirmation of his theses.

Thus, armed only with his conscience and the feeling of the mortality of his results, the scientist finds himself alongside the philosopher in a completely secularized vision of knowledge. United on a voyage with an unknown destination, both have consigned to the archives the dream of the *grand tour*, the myth of origins, and the myth of a single, primordial foundation. Now the adventure of the *detour* begins, a restless wandering along the edge of an ever-mobile frontier, that never ceases to disarrange and recompose the profile of a new history.

1

Twentieth-Century Logic

Willard Van Orman Quine

In 1965, only five years after its publication, Willard Van Orman Quine's *Word and Object* was described by critics as "the most discussed book of American philosophy since the Second World War." Born in 1908 in Akron, Ohio, Quine had long since entered full maturity, and had for some decades played a key role in international philosophy. Having guided the emigration of the ideas and the authors of the Vienna Circle onto American soil at the dawn of the Second World War, he imposed on them a decisive theoretical turn, based on indigenous pragmatism and behaviorism.

The itinerary that led Quine to Vienna and to logical positivism in 1933 was a progressive march towards the East: from the Great Plains through Harvard University, where in only two years he completed a doctorate in mathematical logic under the guidance of Alfred N. Whitehead, co-author with Bertrand Russell of *Principia Mathematica*. His sojourns in Vienna, and then in Prague, brought him into contact with all the great masters of the Vienna Circle, from Rudolf Carnap to Hans Reichenbach, and from Moritz Schlick to the Polish mathematician Alfred Tarski. This contact rapidly became a profound intellectual syntony that, from then onward, would tie Quine to the fate of logical positivism and which, through him, would change the destiny of contemporary American thought. From the citadel of Harvard, where he still remains after forty years of teaching, Quine has never ceased to project an aura of very powerful thought, representing one of the fundamental reference points for the currents of analytic and post-analytic philosophy.

Upon his return from Europe in 1934, and for the following ten years, Quine's contributions were worked out in the articulation of one of the central themes of the internal discussion of the Vienna Circle: the role of logic in the foundation of mathematics, which, from the point of view of some developments in set theory, lies at the center of the article "New Foundations for Mathematical Logic" (1937), not to mention the subsequent volume *Mathematical Logic* (1940). Thanks to Quine, the site of this first theoretical elaboration remained the Harvard campus which, starting in 1939, attracted the masters of European logic, including Carnap, Russell, and Tarski. Some of them, for political and racial reasons, would settle permanently in the United States.

After the war, during which Quine decided to enroll for three years as a volunteer in the Navy and resolved not to read "a single line of philosophy," the publication of the article "Two Dogmas of Empiricism" acted as a genuine detonator for post-analytic philosophy. In this article Quine tried to undermine two main points of Viennese positivism, among them the fundamental distinction between analytic and synthetic propositions, on which the scientific pretensions of the entire positivist discourse were based.

According to the authors of the Circle, analytic propositions are the only ones on which the production of objective knowledge can be founded. In fact, since they lack empirical content (for example, "if it is raining, then it is raining"), they are the only necessarily true assertions. Analytic truth, without saying anything about reality, is founded on a series of syntactic-semantic properties of language. In contrast, synthetic propositions are *a posteriori* and contingent assertions. In fact, the truth of propositions of the type "in such a place at such a time it rains" depends, aside from linguistic factors, on the reality on which they are based.

On the basis of pragmatism, hinging on the "holistic character of experimental control," Quine's critique suggests that a net distinction between these two logical orders is incapable of definition. It is a given that synthetic judgments are true only in relation to the fact that the world is a certain way, that each of them is a case in itself, and that the generalizations must be collectively examined on the basis of individually verifiable consequences. But it is not a given that analytic judgments, even if they can be organized into systems such as logic and mathematics and do not depend on empirical reality, are based on a form of pure logic. The truth of the purely logical proposition "every x is an x" derives from the fact that x neither is nor implies anything, while the truth of the proposition "every bachelor is an unmarried man" depends more on the significance of its constitutive terminology than on purely logical form. Hence the need to redefine the notion of analyticity through the concept of synonymy which, nevertheless, is unable, according to Quine, to restore such a clear and irrefutable distinction. The criteria for distinguishing between the analytic and the synthetic therefore remain pragmatical.

From the article "Two Dogmas of Empiricism" (1951) to the publication in 1960 of *Word and Object*, Quine continued to elaborate his theory of language. Of essential importance in these years was his proximity to the Harvard master of behaviorism, the psychologist B. F. Skinner. Through him, Quine developed a behavioral theory of language acquisition, from which is derived one of his most discussed and original theses, on the "indeterminacy of translation." In this thesis Quine holds that, paradoxically, it would be possible to formulate "manuals of translation," diverse and incompatible among themselves, each of which corresponds to the communicative dispositions of its interlocutor's mother-tongue.

These conclusions induced Quine to recover an aspect of logical discourse banished by the Vienna Circle: that of ontology. According to Carnap, because of the analytic/synthetic, internal/external distinction, the scientist investigated the world and the philosopher deepened the logical structure of the language describing the world. Quine, on the contrary, has declared rationally incongruous the practice of accepting that a system is explicative and irreducible, while at the same time rejecting its constitutive entities. Above all, starting with the essay "Ontological Relativity" (1969), Quine has developed a true ontological theory, based on the idea that ontological inquiry is to be kept to a minimum: that is, to the indispensable minimum necessary for a system to be proved explicative and irreducible.

*

Due to the historical impact of your theories, you are referred to as the "father" of post–World War II American philosophy, but in what way do you feel like the "son" of United States culture?

Mathematical logic, my true passion, wasn't popular on this side of the Atlantic; its centers at the end of last century were on both sides of the Alps, Germany and Italy. In 1910 and '11 Russell and Whitehead's *Principia Mathematica* was not very influential in the United States. Until World War II, the centers for this new discipline were Germany, Poland, and, partly, Austria, thanks to the emblematic figure of Kurt Gödel. Alonzo Church played an important role in the diffusion of mathematical logic in the United States, and it was also thanks to him that, after his return to the U.S. in 1932 having completed a Ph.D. at Göttingen, the discipline became widespread in American philosophy departments. I came back from Europe a year after him, and we were the first ones to promote mathematical logic—Church from Princeton, and I from Harvard. In the years that followed, before and after the war, a great number of émigrés, exiles, and political refugees made the United States the center of mathematical logic.

If your interest in mathematical logic is not common in the American context, what was the origin of your interest in such an abstract subject, one that seems almost mystical, like a form of transcendental meditation on the conditions of thought?

It's a story of a funny coincidence, as it always is in life. When I was in college I was undecided among three majors: philosophy, mathematics, and linguistics. By chance, an older student mentioned *Mathematical Philosophy*, by Bertrand Russell, and it was love at first sight. It was possible to join all my interests in one. I decided to major in mathematics, and I did my honors reading in philosophy of mathematics, which eventually became mathematical logic.

Hence, Russell was your point of departure.

Yes, and along with him were Boole, and even Giuseppe Peano, whose *Formulario Matematico* I had first read in French.

And the logicians of the American tradition, such as Charles Sanders Peirce?

I missed Peirce at first. I'm not sure I had even heard of him when I was in college. He didn't happen to get onto the reading list that my professor had made up for me. When I came down here to Harvard to pursue my graduate studies, I began to find out about

Peirce. Georges Sardon, the editor of a history of science quarterly called *Isis*, asked me to review the volumes on logic in Peirce's *Collected Papers*, which were just beginning to be published by Harvard University Press. I reviewed volumes two, three, and four of Peirce's work, and thus learned about him, but I didn't really gain that much in the way of logical content. What I learned about was historical perspective.

How do you relate to the pragmatist tradition of which Peirce, along with William James and John Dewey, can be considered the forerunners?

It's hard to say what constitutes pragmatism. If one considers it a branch of the empiricist tradition then yes, it is very important for me. Here at Harvard my teacher Clarence Irving Lewis called himself a "conceptual pragmatist." Before I went to college, I read William James's *Pragmatism* by chance, since my brother had sent it to me. Then, during my graduate studies at Cambridge, I read a lot by Hume, Locke, and Berkeley. But I don't think that the influence on me was distinctively American; it was rather one of international empiricism. It was in fact Whitehead, Rudolf Carnap, C. I. Lewis, and, among the Poles, Tarski, who influenced me a great deal. I suppose that I think of philosophy more horizontally than vertically.

About Whitehead: in Italy he was a very important author within the "Husserl Renaissance," inaugurated by Enzo Paci in the fifties. And I would say that Whitehead was better known as a "philosopher of relationism" than as a logician.

I met Whitehead at Harvard toward the end of the twenties when he was better known as co-author of Russell's *Principia Mathematica* than for his own work. I did my Ph.D. thesis under Whitehead's sponsorship. When I met him, he wasn't working in logic anymore, but he was lecturing in process and reality, and had already written *Process and Reality* and *Science in the Modern World*. I attended his lectures and was very impressed by his wisdom, but I learned more, philosophically, from C. I. Lewis. However, my big gains were after I got my Ph.D. and went to Europe on a fellowship in 1932. That's where I caught up with Rudolf Carnap, at the Vienna Circle meetings first, and then in Prague.

What do you remember of your first meeting with Carnap?

We were very congenial from the beginning. Carnap was very hospitable and generous and went out of his way to find a place for my wife and me to stay in Prague. I went to his lectures and, when he wasn't lecturing, I would go out to where he lived at the edge of the city and talk with him for hours. I was reading his new book, which was still being typed by his wife, and I would take the new pages with me and study them, in order to discuss them with him when I returned. We argued and discussed these things and it was a tremendously fruitful period for me. I became quite a devotee of Carnap's philosophy until, over the next few years, I began to see difficulties with his work, and my own ideas diverged from his. He also saw difficulties in it and changed his views, but we changed our views on his initial position in different ways. There was a fair amount of debate between us in our correspondence, soon to be published by the University of California Press. We continued to be good friends right to the end, and, although we disagreed on certain points, I gained more from Carnap than from any other philosopher.

Who else did you meet in the Vienna Circle?

In Prague I met Philip Frank, who later came to Harvard. In Vienna I met Moritz Schlick, Friedrich Waismann, and Kurt Gödel, whose great discovery had just been published. What I learned in Vienna was due to my fluency in German, which was also of great value to me in Prague with Carnap. In Warsaw at the time there was primarily mathematical logic, even though, eventually, it transformed itself into a proper philosophy of logic. In Prague, a purely philosophical enthusiasm reigned, thanks to Carnap. All of this, of course, was happening before the Nazis.

What was the impact of Nazism on this school of thought?

Everyone I knew was horrified from the very start, before the Holocaust, before any of the unthinkable things happened. The antisemitism in Vienna was evident before the Nazis took power. There were Nazi demonstrations, graffiti on the walls against Jews, and when the Nazis took over there were scandalous moves, like when they dismissed Einstein from the Prussian Academy. The Nazis also founded an outrageously racist mathematical quarterly, *Deutsche Mathematik*. They were allowed to re-occupy the Rhineland: it was so clear that we should take a firm stand about the gravity of the situation. In 1938 I was in Portugal for half a year, and my friends there talked about their discouragement with the British attitude of appeasement, and with Chamberlain. I didn't know anybody, even back then, who wasn't worried and outraged by the Nazis. When I hear that people didn't realize the extent of depravation under the Nazis, I don't believe it. Of course we couldn't forsee how bad it was going to be, and we didn't have details about extermination camps. But you could feel an extreme nationalism, and there were many who were very sympathetic to the idea of a reinvigorated Germany. There were a lot of stupid people, and there were a lot of rather evil people. I was eager for the United States to get into the war.

What was your position on the political situation? Did you support any sort of "social engagement"?

More than a position, mine was a reaction. I volunteered in the Navy, where I became an officer. I wasn't liable for the draft because of my age and my position here at Harvard; there were special concessions for teachers. I felt that Western culture was on the verge of collapse, and all I was doing was philosophy of logic. That was certainly the sort of thing that could be put aside. I didn't read a line of philosophy or logic for three years.

This happened after 1939, which you have described as a great year for Harvard's philosophy department, where Bertrand Russell, Alfred Tarski, Carnap, and the Vienna Circle were guests.

I returned in the fall of 1933 and was appointed junior fellow at the Society of Fellows at Harvard. In 1938 I became an instructor, and I've been here ever since. Carnap came over on the occasion of Harvard's tricentenary, in 1934. I had given several public lectures on Carnap, and I hoped that Harvard would hire him, but we didn't swing it; he was hired by the University of Chicago. But we had good times when Carnap was in this part of the world. Tarski arrived in 1939 and we found him a job at City College in New York. 'Thirty-eight to '41 were splendid years.

What was Russell's role in this context?

I had met Russell earlier and had corresponded with him for years. He came to Harvard in 1931 to give lectures. Whitehead introduced him to the audience and he also introduced him to me. When my first book, *A System of Logistic,* was published in 1934, I sent Russell a copy. He was a very open man. I jealously save many of his letters with compliments and objections concerning that first book of mine. I owe a great deal to Russell, to his logic, and also to his philosophy, especially his books: *Our Knowledge of the External World,* his introduction to *Mathematical Philosophy,* and, of course, to *Principia Mathematica.*

Russell was not only a logician but also one of the philosophers who, in the tradition of our century, demonstrated more interest in the great political and social events. His pacifist faith even brought him to jail during the First World War, and then the Russell Tribunal attracted worldwide attention to the American intervention in Vietnam.

I was never drawn to socialism and communism as he was, much less to the views he held in his declining years when he was demonstrating against the United States in favor of Soviet Russia. Until the Nazi alarm I hadn't been politically active or conscious. I would neglect newspapers for days, but I began to read them again in '32.

During your stay in Vienna, phenomenology was a flourishing field of study. Three years before your arrival in Austria, Edmund Husserl published his *Formal and Transcendental Logic* (1929), and in Freiburg his favorite student and successor, Martin Heidegger, was working on *What is Metaphysics?* expediting the detachment of existentialism from phenomenology.

The phenomenological tradition never attracted me very much. I read Husserl's *Logical Investigations* with difficulty, but I couldn't get into the rules of the game; much of it was a matter of introspection, and his terms seemed vague to me. Somebody has tried to establish some link between my philosophy and his phenomenology. I was never too convinced, though I recognize that Husserl and I, in very different ways, addressed some of the same things. I am interested in the combination of behaviorism and neurology, and he was interested in introspection.

Behaviorism has been interpreted as a variant of pragmatism in social sciences like pedagogy, sociology, and psychology. What has it meant to a logician with a mathematical background like you?

Behaviorism has always been important for me. Stetson, my psychology professor in college, assigned John B. Watson's *Psychology from the Standpoint of the Behaviorist*. Then, when I was a junior fellow here at Harvard in 1933–36, I came to know Burrhus F. Skinner, who was a junior fellow also. We became great friends, we talked a great deal, we both felt that we were behaviorists when we met. However, I believe that behaviorism isn't ultimately explanatory, though it is indispensable methodologically. What is important is to consider the neurological mechanism for some introspectively identified mental state, or mental process. You need to specify that process in objectively verifiable and recognizable terms, so you need behavioral criteria to set the problem for which you are going to look to neurology for the solution. It is the same in medicine. In the case of an infectious disease you look for the micro-organism but you don't identify the disease by that organism, you identify the disease by the symptoms. Verbal behavior is the symptom: it comprises the symptoms of mental states, just as symptoms of a medical sort provide the criteria for finding the micro-organism that is the cause.

How does your position differ from classical behaviorism, and from Skinner in particular?

Skinner and I share the fundamental position that an explanation—not the deepest one, but one of a shallower kind—is possible at the purest behavioral level. One can hope to find, and I think one does find, behavioral regularities. In economics, for instance, you can formulate the concept of unemployment without reducing the phenomenon of economics to the behavior of individual people, which would be unproductive and chaotic. The instructive regularities occur at another level. In psychology that level is behaviorism.

Your idea that there exists a set of integrable recurrences, from the smallest to the biggest, seems to belong to the organicist matrix. In fact, to define your horizon of thought, you bring to the field a concept very close to that of organicism: a philosophical "holism," by which any organism, biological or physical, must be understood as an organized totality rather then as the sum of its discrete parts.

Holism is a convergence of various hypotheses, theories, beliefs, truths; even when one focuses on any one of these, the others have to help. Carnap shows his appreciation of this by speaking well of Pierre Duhem, who with Poincaré and Milhaud, founded conventionalism. Carnap, like others in the Vienna Circle, didn't follow the consequences of holism sufficiently: they appreciated that further hypotheses might be drawn supporting their thesis, but they overlooked the fact that, when you take hypotheses seriously, not only is the effort great, but it is also embedded with practical consequences. Even in mathematics, arithmetic, and differential calculus, the laws can be made to be operative: those laws are part of the holistic bundle that implies from the start the experimental result— your predictions. Hence one can avoid Carnap's dilemma of trying to explain how mathematics could be meaningful, since it was devoid of content. Furthermore, it even helps explain the necessity of mathematical truth, which Carnap tried to explain with the concept of "analyticity," so closely bound up with the notion of "syntheticity," its contrary.

The renewal of the holistic perspective, then, marked the most decisive moment of your separation from Carnap and from the logical positivists.

Certainly it marked my separation from Carnap. I have actually tempered the extreme holism of my first writings. If one accepts the holistic hypothesis, the conclusion is that, except for logic and mathematics, there is only one science. On the contrary, beyond logic and mathematics there isn't only extravagance. The way I look at things today is that there isn't only one science, but a big enough bundle of laws not to be comprehended in a single hypothesis. The big enough bundle implies logically some observational conditions, namely some categories defining observable situations. The connection between science and observation is made through these categoricals, and holism is needed to the extent that you have a big enough combination to apply some of these testable categories.

Your interest in ontology suggests a detachment from the analytic philosophy derived from Carnap and the neo-positivism which remains your major point of reference. Why is it that after the Second World War this current of thought, so different from pragmatism and any preceding American tradition, has had so much success in the United States?

The United States was strongly influenced by both the English tradition and the very different tradition of analytic philosophy that came from Vienna. I belonged to the Vienna side, through Wittgenstein and his followers, but John Austin and Peter Strawson also had a strong influence on me. Bertrand Russell was naturally very important: he was like a bridge between the two schools, and he had a strong influence on Wittgenstein. In the United States, Russell was absorbed partly through Vienna and partly through British analytic philosophy. Between the wars, the scientific temper in America was intensified by the influx of European scientists from Germany and Austria.

Don't you think that for Americans still fascinated by the New Deal, the Viennese émigrés also represented a liberal and liberating form of thought, antagonistic to that historicist imposition often seen in the background of totalitarian ideologies?

That's partially true. I think that an anti-historicist mood was prevalent in the United States before their arrival. For me the scientific motivation was dominant. Ever since the beginning there had always been a great exchange between the scientists and the philosophers of the Vienna Circle. Philip Frank, who had emigrated to the U.S. in 1936, took over Einstein's position at Princeton, and this brought Carnap there a few times. We were reading the same texts and teaching the same authors.

Following the detachment from logical positivism and analytic philosophy, your thought has sometimes been defined in a "post-analytic" perspective. If you had to think about any other post-analytic philosopher, whom would you name?

Donald Davidson comes close. Also, Roger Gibson, and, to some extent, Hilary Putnam. I can't exclude Nelson Goodman, with whom I have also worked. Goodman was a graduate student when

I was still an instructor at Harvard. We would get together periodically for an evening and discuss philosophical problems. That was a very good thing, but then he went to Penn, where he remained for many years. In any case, I feel the same intellectual empathy with Europe as I do with the U.S., although, in the European context, England is a different story. Although I spent two years at Oxford and I have many friends there, I don't feel England has had a great impact on my work.

Going back to the thirties, to Vienna and to your first European trip, do you remember if there were any exchanges between the Vienna Circle and the literary and art world?

No, actually I was only in contact with philosophers. I attended Schlick's lectures on the theory of knowledge, a subject I was very interested in at the time. However, the main value for me was the practice in language because, as I said before, German was so useful later with Carnap and the Poles.

And in other moments in your life, has art ever been a support or an inspiration?

As a young man, I was fascinated by a literary piece that certainly was a factor in my becoming interested in philosophy: Edgar Allan Poe's *Eureka*. I read all of Poe. When I read him again years later, I found it outrageous. There was cosmology modeled on nineteenth-century astronomy—a very old view of reality and the universe. I was fascinated by the cosmological conjectures about the origins of planets. The combination of the grandeur of the whole picture painted by Poe, and the grandiose language in which he presented it, fascinated me. I was interested in writing, and tried to write in the style of Poe. I even considered a career in writing. But, by the time I was in college, I had stronger interests in mathematics and philosophy, and my idea of becoming a writer brought me to another kind of writing.

How did the jump from Poe to mathematical logic take place?

My interest in science was as strong as my interest in philosophy. They both involved reality and the universe. Theoretical physicists study the philosophical reasons of the universe. If I hadn't hated the experimental side of physics, I could have become a physicist. I am mechanophobic; I am terribly afraid of machines.

Your words make me think about the origins of philosophy and about the great pre-Socratic physicists, Thales, Anaximenes, Anaximander. Cosmologists and navigators at the same time. Children of a great navigational culture, the Greek one, which is, after all, like the American one: it suffices to think of Melville.

I'm very keen on travel, from way back. Traveling means crossing cultural and mental boundaries. I've lectured on six continents, I've visited a hundred and thirteen countries. This may have something to do with alternating generations in my family. My father had a true passion for machines but he didn't travel at all, except on business. His father, on the other hand, was a sailor. Perhaps I, too, am a bit of sailor: a sailor of logic.

2

Post-Analytic Visions
Donald Davidson

The charm of philosopher Donald Davidson lies in the rigor of his research, a work of patient and creative deconstruction dedicated for more than thirty years to that language, half analytic and half post-analytic, that is at the base of the work of Willard Van Orman Quine. The Harvard campus, located only a few miles from Springfield, where he was born in 1917, was the scene of the meeting between the young Davidson and Quine, master and never-ceasing friend of intellectual challenge. It was the dawn of the Second World War, during which Davidson, like Quine, decided to sign up as volunteer in the Navy, serving from 1942 to 1945.

After the war, in Quine's seminars, Davidson learned of a new thematic horizon of philosophy that, under the guidance of the late Alfred North Whitehead, had until then been identified in a terrain very close to the history of ideas. His thesis on Plato's *Philebus* bears witness to this first phase, which nonetheless left not a few traces in his subsequent work as a post-analytic philosopher.

The operation conducted by Davidson on the theoretical horizon opened by Quine reveals itself in a series of essays that have been collected in two volumes: in 1980, under the title *Essays on Actions and Events,* and in 1984, as *Inquiries into Truth and Interpretation.* In its basic intention, Davidson's work can be defined as the attempt to include in the singularly "perceptive" universe of empiricism the ethical and linguistic question of intersubjectivity. As Richard Rorty has observed, Davidson has preserved the logic from Quine's logical empiricism while abandoning the empiricism. Put another way, this signifies that Davidson, even in preserving the attention to language inaugurated by Quine, does not subscribe to the epistemology, which is still completely rooted in the perceptive solipsism typical of the empiricist subject.

Davidson maintains that there survives in Quine, as in Rudolf Carnap and in many other empiricists, a Cartesian tendency that consists in believing that each of us can "construct" the world as it is given to the perceptive senses. This presupposes that language, or the mind, "organizes" the reality of the senses according to determined conceptual schemes. On the contrary, both language and the mind are part, along with the world, of a single conceptual scheme, an intersubjective matrix and process. For Davidson it is not possible to lose the faculty of speaking a language while at the same time maintaining any capacity to think. All reality, subjective and objective, is uniformly constituted and nourished by language and interpretation.

Davidson admits that Quine salvaged the possibility of a philosophy of language, freeing it from a weighty "dogma" of empiricism: the distinction between analytic and synthetic propositions, or between the architectonics of thought, on one side, and the content of thought on the other. Without the "pragmatic" option of being able to choose a conceptual scheme on the basis of its greater efficiency with respect to the contingent objectives of research, philosophy could not have continued in the way it has. But in his attempt "to render empiricism scientifically acceptable," Quine is not exempt from proposing a third dogma: that of a perceptive solipsism, a true *privacy of the mind.*

There are no purely subjective perceptions or reactions that can be identified as points of primogenitive departure and subsequently organized within a mental framework. Nothing in the world is the result of pure nervous stimulation; everything is "situation" or "event," which depends upon our being in constant communication with other people, individuals and objects, with which we are integrated in the same context of meaning.

Thought depends on a triangular configuration of relations involving at least two interlocutors and a series of shared events. What is given to the individual is not, in the last instance, the sensory organs; rather, it is this communicative triangulation. It is not perception, but intersubjectivity and interpretation that are at the basis of knowledge.

Hence I have asked Davidson what separates him from the interactive perception of pragmatism. All the more so since even its most recent voice, Richard Rorty, has wanted to recognize in him a fellow traveler. In fact, the communicative process, understood as the reaching of a consensus by a specific social or scientific community, has always lain at the basis of thought in the pragmatist tradition, from Charles S. Peirce to Clarence I. Lewis. For Davidson, on the contrary, the notion of consensus remains secondary, and precisely herein lies his fundamental originality in comparison with the pragmatist perspective. Intersubjectivity is the root of thought, in the sense of its transcendental condition, which therefore does not require the production of a consensus. Speaking of consensus means presupposing that ideas exist prior to the consensus, and that these ideas, when confronted with other ideas, bring about an agreement. In Davidson's mind, language, understood as the intersubjective production of meanings, comes before everything: before sharing in a vision of the world, ideas do not exist.

*

To the European eye, you represent the prototype of the American postwar philosopher, with your strictly analytic training, an itinerary faithful to itself, built step-by-step along a disciplinary trajectory, sheltered from historical and social disturbances. . .

The awareness of belonging to a particular tradition comes with time. When one is young, one doesn't care very much. I studied at Harvard, both as an undergraduate and as a graduate student, and the first philosopher that influenced me was Whitehead, who was English and had moved to America. Whitehead's philosophy, in retrospect, doesn't seem to have been in any particular tradition; he was very historically minded—he seemed unrelated even to Russell, with whom he had worked on *Principia Mathematica*—his philosophy was very much his own work. Whitehead's views fitted very well with my tastes in philosophy, because they were extremely metaphysical in character and geared to his idea of the history of thought. At the time, my interests were more literary than philosophical. It was only toward the end of my undergraduate time that I became seriously interested in philosophy as opposed to, let's say, just the history of ideas.

When did the meeting with Quine take place?

It was at the end of my undergraduate career and early in my graduate career that I met Quine. He was then more or less fresh back from Europe, where he had met the Polish philosophers as well as the Austrian and German philosophers, by whom he had been greatly influenced. He was lecturing about them. Quine changed the focus of my interests, though I continued to work in classical philosophy and wrote my dissertation on Plato. If you had asked me how I saw the historical situation that I was in then, as opposed to how I see it now, the answer would be quite different. But the easiest way is to look back. The biggest intellectual influence on me was certainly Quine, but C. I. Lewis was also important.

Lewis is a pragmatist thinker, relatively unknown in Europe, but cited by Quine as a cardinal point of reference.

As I see it now, Lewis had a tremendous influence on Quine. Lewis combined an interest in logic with a kind of mixture of British empiricism and Kant, which he managed to put together with a strong dash of American pragmatism That's really a way of describing Quine's philosophical position, though I doubt it would be Quine's way of describing it. He would recognize the influence of pragmatism and British empiricism, but he would deny the Kantian element, which comes from Lewis and which demarcates the difference in our present position. I think that Lewis's influence is perhaps less clear in Quine than in me. Lewis was a Kant scholar and an important epistemologist in his own right. It is very clear that the mixture of Kant and Pragmatism goes back to Dewey, who picked it up directly in Europe. I see a sort of historical development from post-Kantian philosophy in Germany to pragmatism, as they are combined in Dewey and, to a certain extent, in Peirce. This was then picked up by Lewis and then Quine.

In this sense, you don't identify a distinctly American line of thought?

No, the only peculiarly American line of thought is pragmatism. But I do not have as keen a sense of what pragmatism did to philosophy as, let's say, Rorty does. Rorty claims that I'm a pragmatist.

Don't you consider yourself a pragmatist?

No. I don't disbelieve in it, but I don't particularly understand what Rorty means by that, because for him that's a special kind of anti-metaphysical attitude. At one time, he actually had a pragmatic theory of truth, and then dropped it. I remember one of his articles, called "Truth, Pragmatism, and Davidson," in which he explains what he means by calling me a pragmatist. But part of what he has in mind is just that I seem to have dropped the attempt to get a certain definition of the notion of truth. I've certainly dropped the idea that philosophers are in charge of a special sort of truth. But I don't think of that as being any more pragmatic than a lot of other positions.

Isn't it somewhat true that both you and Quine—though he more so than you—tend to *un*learn the pragmatist influence in favor of the European tradition that stretches from Carnap, Reichenbach, and the authors of the Vienna Circle to Tarski and the Polish logicians?

The important thing in Quine, and certainly in me too, is abandoning the analytic/synthetic distinction. And Quine could not have failed to recognize in this an element of pragmatism. We choose our conceptual scheme according to what seems to fit best the type of science we're doing. This is what separates Quine from the European logical positivists, who have otherwise had a huge influence on him, and through him, on me.

This is an important point, that the demolition of the distinction between analytic and synthetic has a pragmatist basis.

To deny the analytic/synthetic distinction is to suppose that you cannot make a strong division between the architectonics of thought and its content. You can choose your own structure, which was already Lewis's idea. But Lewis retained the analytic/synthetic distinction, so the connection is not as simple as I made it sound. Lewis was a pragmatist about the sort of conceptual scheme that one chooses, but once it's chosen, he kept operating within the strong distinction between the analytic and synthetic. Indeed, this was also true for Carnap, who thought that one could choose one's own ethos in terms of languages, choose one's own language as one pleased—but that having chosen a language one had thereby chosen where to draw the line between analytic and synthetic. It was

Quine's original inspiration to ask, once somebody has got a language and a theory, how do you decide where he has drawn the line? This is surely one of Quine's most influential inventions, or let's say, intellectual breakthroughs. It changes the whole way one thinks about language and thought.

You would then be more keen to identify yourself in a Western rather than in a specifically American tradition?

You have to bear in mind that the logical positivists were having a tremendous influence in the U.S. just at the time that I was a graduate student. During, just before, and just after the war, all these people came to the United States, and it was impossible not to be influenced by them.

In light of the path American philosophy followed in subsequent decades, why did logical positivism impose itself hegemonically in the United States, rather than other European movements such as phenomenology or the Frankfurt school?

Well, for one thing, many of the logical positivists were in Austria, where life became extremely uncomfortable. They weren't necessarily Jewish, some were and some were not. Some of them were married to Jews, for example Carl Hempel. There simply wasn't an intellectual climate, and many of them went to England first and then settled in the United States. Also, there were many bright young Americans who went to England for one or more years, and perhaps got a degree at Oxford. They were influenced by Wittgenstein and Russell, who was already widely read and who was soon to come to the United States. I was not one of the people who went to England. I didn't go until quite late in my thirties, sometime in the 1950s, and by that time my philosophical views were pretty well formed. So I wasn't tremendously influenced by what was going on there. However, before I went to England I was an avid reader of people like Ryle, Austin, and Strawson.

Don't you think that there is a sort of structural bifurcation within the panorama of Anglo-American analytic philosophy, constituted by the persistence of two distinct and conflicting schools of thought: on the one hand, the English tradition, inaugurated by Russell and Wittgenstein and dedicated to the analy-

sis of "ordinary language"; and, on the other hand, a more formalistic tradition of Austrian origin, begun by Carnap and the
Vienna Circle and then mutated by the American analytic
current?

It depends on what you mean by analytic philosophy. If you think
of analytic philosophy as being characterized by an interest in a
scientific method and in logic, then that certainly came more from
the Continent than it did from England. In retrospect, I see that I
had been influenced by both the positivists, with their interest in
scientific method and logic, and by the school—or better yet, the
movement—of "ordinary language," which was in the atmosphere
in England. I had not yet been to either Europe or England, but I
was influenced by the things I was reading. If you were to look
back at my first influential article, "Actions, Reasons, and Causes,"
I think you'd be struck by the fact that it combines these two elements in a way that was not very common at the time. For me, the
origin of ideas is a retrospective issue. When I started writing, I
never really asked myself where my work fits in, I simply did what
interested me and let other people worry about where it came from.

**Your first theoretical operation was therefore to reconcile the
Viennese formalism with the English "ordinary language"
movement.**

Looking back, I'd say that would be a way of characterizing it, but
at the time it would not have been my objective. You realize that I
didn't start publishing until I was quite old. My first published work
was done at Stanford, and it was done in collaboration with Patrick
Suppies and J. C. MacKinsey. They got me interested in some mildly
technical aspects of decision theory, which belongs as much to
psychology and economics as it does to philosophy, and that work
has had a big influence on me ever since. If you were to ask me
where that influence came from, I would say that one major element
was Alfred Tarski, not that I was a student of his, but he had a
tremendous influence on Suppies and on MacKinsey, who influenced me. That is the origin of my interest in semantics, which
some people see as the most original contribution of my work. As
you can see, in those years there wasn't just the dualism between
Continental philosophy and Anglo-American philosophy, but a
more articulated network of influences.

From the point of view of a historian of philosophy, what makes
you stand out most among the protagonists on the American
scene is the central role you attribute to the notion of intersubjectivity. In fact, you were the first to use this concept in the
post-empiricist epistemological frame inaugurated by Quine.

My discussion of intersubjectivity is connected to my attempt to
systematize semantics. On the one hand, with semantics we see how
to construct a formal theory for at least a large fragment of the
natural languages. The related task is to ask how to tell when such
a theory fits the normal behavior of some individual or group of
individuals. At this point you get down to applications. I see the
work in philosophy of language, indeed in the philosophy of mind
in general, as a matter of having a comprehensive theory not only
for language, but also for other propositional attitudes, like belief
and so on. The other part of it is speculating on how you can tell
that such a theory fits the behavior of some person or group. The
first part is what I call the "spinning of a theory," to see what kind
of a formal structure language and thought constitute. The other
part, which deals with the capacity of theory to reflect social behavior, implies the notion of interpretation The important question
then becomes: whom, if anybody, does this theory interpret?

Don't you think that these affirmations emphasize your pragmatism, in the presence of, for example, Quine?

No, because Quine did not put the question in quite the same way
that I am putting it, because he put much less emphasis on the
theory as far as language is concerned. It was Quine who, above
all, asked the question, what is the empirical evidence by which
somebody means so and so by what they say? Word and Object is
the first big work on that topic from the point of view of somebody
who didn't take for granted that he knew what meanings were,
but tried to reconceive the problem of understanding the nature of
communication without using inherited categories like synonymy
and analyticity and meaning.

This is true. But if I asked the question in a more direct way,
"Who is more pragmatist, Davidson or Quine?" what would you
answer? It is difficult to maintain the view that the category of

intersubjectivity, first introduced into this universe of discourse by you, does not imply a pragmatic dimension.

I don't know what my notion of intersubjectivity has to do with pragmatism. There was one early pragmatist, named Mead, who was at the University of Chicago, and who was as much of an anthropologist as he was a philosopher. But he did have the idea that, somehow, not only meaning, but thought itself emerged only in the context of intersubjective relations. As far as I know, I certainly didn't get this idea from Mead because, although I had read a little bit of Mead while I was in graduate school, I did not retain it.

But this idea wasn't just Mead's.

It's an idea that was common among the pragmatists, including Dewey. The idea that thought itself is possible only in the context of having a language, an intersubjective communication with others, is certainly an idea that has been growing on me for the last fifteen years or more. The way I see it now is that thought identifies with propositional attitudes, in the sense of "perceiving" or "feeling" things are "this or that" way. This notion of thinking implies interdependence in the sense that you cannot attribute propositional content to creatures that don't have speech. At first, I just tried to argue for this by saying that there was no reason to say that a creature had the concept of the way things seem, as opposed to the way things are, unless there was intersubjective communication. More recently, I have argued for this more directly by saying that the whole idea that one's reactions are to objects in the world, situations and events, rather than, let's say, just responses to stimulation of nerve endings, depends on our being in communication with other people who are interacting with the same things. Obviously, what allows our interaction with other people is not based on the stimulations of our nerve endings, or anything subjective at all, but on the events to which we are exposed in the outside world.

It may be that my European eye focuses too much on debts and genealogies, but I think that all this is very pragmatistic.

I don't know how much of that is in the pragmatists. I think some of it is in Mead, and it is also true that for Dewey language and thought have social functions. I have looked through these people for arguments, but I haven't discovered any. I've been trying to understand the reasons this must be the case, and what I have found is that it is almost a commonplace among American pragmatists that thought and language go together, but what I haven't found is much or any argument for that case.

What do you think of the neo-pragmatist reading of your work proposed by Richard Rorty?

Owing something to pragmatism is not one of my obsessions. I have the general feeling that I might well have been influenced by the pragmatists, and I certainly was by Quine's and Lewis's pragmatism. But if I go back, as I have done often in recent years, to the pragmatists themselves, I find it very hard to read them, part of the reason being that they weren't much given to argument. Dewey, who was terrific in his way, hardly ever bothered to give reasons for what he said; he would just tell you what he thought and it was often good stuff. But that is not the way I do philosophy.

Then, the work of philosophy is to give "reasons" and argumentations appropriate to specific positions?

I maintain that thought itself absolutely depends on a three-way relationship between at least two people and a series of events that are shared in the world. Although I am aware that this seems a commonplace of one's ordinary intuitive picture of how language is learned, it hasn't been taken all that seriously by philosophers.

The metaphor of the triangle, constituted by two interlocutors and an ensemble of experiences shared through communication is one of the common grounds that Quine would not recognize. The reason for this lies in what you defined as the "Cartesian" background, that is, the condition of privacy of the mind in which Quine's empiricist "I" operates.

Quine wants to start with what is given to the individual. His idea is to start with our sense organs and build everything from there, and that is what Descartes and the empiricists have in common. I don't agree with this premise. I don't think we can make clear sense of the idea that whatever happens at our nerve endings has some special epistemological significance. Here I see the relationship between Dewey and myself, because Dewey also was an anti-empiricist in this sense. He thought that we learn by moving along and interacting with things in the world. I agree that each of us works out a world picture by himself, and then, with luck, we share it with someone else. But I add that we do not have a formed picture until we are in communication with somebody else.

Then, in a certain sense, you radicalize Dewey's "interactive" point of view. For you, it is no longer sufficient to maintain, like the pragmatists, that one can have knowledge only from the moment in which the single vision of the world is shared, but you insist that it is not possible to reach a vision of the world in the first place without intersubjective sharing.

Look, what I call the "Cartesian vision" is just a metaphor, and not a comment on Descartes. There is one way of doing philosophy in which you suppose that something is presented to us. That something is either raw experience, sensory data, or stimulations of our nerve endings—it doesn't make any difference; on the basis of this, we construct a picture of an outside world and of other people. I prefer to call such pictures empirical and Cartesian because we can develop a picture of the world all by ourselves, and we could do so even if there were nobody else in the world. Now, my own view is that, until we have an idea of what's going on in the minds of other people, it doesn't make sense to say that we have the concept of objectivity, of something existing in the world quite independent of us. The empiricists have it exactly backwards, because they think that first one knows what's in his own mind, then, with luck, he finds out what is in the outside world, and, with even more luck, he finds out what is in somebody else's mind. I think differently. First we find out what is in somebody else's mind, and by then we have got all the rest. Of course, I really think that it all comes at the same time.

How would you define the concept of mind in the context of the absolute priority of intersubjectivity?

The mind is nothing more than the brain, and we can characterize people at certain points as having thoughts. The basis of objectivity is intersubjectivity.

But if objectivity does not exist without intersubjectivity, how do you define the space of subjectivity? It is in this sense that I am interested in what you have to say about the mind.

We really can distinguish three different kinds of knowledge. The most important one, the one without which there would not be any other, is third-person knowledge; that is, the knowledge of what is in other minds. The implication is that we have to communicate with somebody else, which means knowing what they are thinking in order to have a concept of objectivity—that is, a concept of objects in a public space and time. Of course, if we have knowledge of other minds, we must at the same time already have a concept of the shared world. Knowledge of the external, in the sense of shared, world, is the second kind of knowledge, from which follows a third: the knowledge of what happens inside ourselves.

Are there differences between these three types of knowledge: that which we can learn from someone else's mind, that of common objects in the world, and that of oneself?

Certainly And to understand them, we need to begin with a question. If we ask what the criteria are for saying that some object is three feet long, the criteria themselves are objective in the sense that we can agree with other people as to what the criteria are. For example, we map lengths of things or temperatures on the basis of numbers, insofar as the relevant properties of numbers is a fact we can agree upon. When it comes to keeping track of what is in somebody else's mind, there is no way to agree on criteria, because our contacts with other minds were the basis of the criteria. So, when we ask, "what does somebody else think, believe, or want?" all we can do is relate their states of mind to our own states of mind. There is only a subjective yardstick. But there is also a mild paradox—that intersubjectivity is the sphere where each of us uses his own thoughts to make sense of other people's thoughts—so that between us we construct something intersubjective that is objective.

Then, knowledge of someone else's mind first comes from knowledge of the outside world.

This is what I take to be the deep difference between the social sciences and the physical sciences. There is a sense in which the yardstick we use is unshared when we talk about other people, whereas when we are talking about the outside world, it is shared. Roughly, external objects are at an equal distance between us and we try to triangulate that. But if we ask ourselves about the type of communication between two minds, the feature is different.

And the third type of knowledge? that of oneself?

The third type of knowledge is the knowledge of our mind, and we cannot talk about criteria anymore. It does not make any sense to ask, "Does my sentence 'the snow is white' really mean that the snow is white?" Self-interpretation does not have criteria, except when you begin to use very sophisticated psychoanalytic and Freudian concepts to question the contents of your own mind from the point of view of other things that are also in your mind. Basically, however, you don't interpret yourself on the basis of evidence. When things go wrong, you act as though you were looking at yourself from the outside.

Now I understand better your anti-Cartesian position.

There is a sense in which I believe we know what is in our minds without having to go through other people. However, I don't think that this is the basis of our knowledge of the external world. The empiricists, as well as the "Cartesianists," agree that what happens in our minds is the point from which we start to build by induction. I don't agree at all.

Could one say that consensus is at the basis of objectivity?

Consensus is the wrong way of putting it, because to speak of consensus makes it sound as though each of us has his own ideas and we come to an agreement, whereas, I am saying that we don't have any ideas until we share a picture of the world. For me, the wrong picture is that each of us has our own ideas and we develop language to find out whether we agree or disagree. It is not until communication springs up that we begin to have ideas. It is not as though we have to reach agreement. Rather, the question is whether we succeed in talking together and thinking together. And if we do, we share a great deal.

Thus you also resolve the problem of pluralism: given the con-
temporaneity of knowledge (thought) and communication (intersubjectivity), one does not presuppose the coexistence of a pluralism of unities. Don't you think that this connection sheds
new light on the relationship, at once interested and distanced,
between you and Jürgen Habermas? For Habermas, in contrast
to you, intersubjectivity is the confrontation of diverse points of
view, while consensus is the objective that all points of view
must reach so as to be able to coexist in reciprocal liberty.

Once we understand each other so that we can have a dialogue,
then we can meaningfully disagree or agree. But agreement and
disagreement depend upon mutual understanding. The point at
which dialectic is possible is the point at which the things I'm taking
seriously have already taken place, because dialogue requires that
you understand one another. Only when you understand one another can you disagree.

My impression is that you take into consideration a more transcendental level of discourse.

That's right. Habermas comes at a later stage, a more important
stage, politically. He thinks about people who understand one another well enough to disagree.

You are often classified as a scholar of semantics rather than as
an epistemologist, especially in relation to Quine. But if I think
about the role you attribute to the concept of intersubjectivity,
and to the "transcendental" level of your philosophical reflection, I don't see the reason for this distinction. You are an epistemologist in every sense.

I think that this classification has been encouraged by Quine. . . . And
I think that what he sees as the difference between epistemology and
semantics, I see as the difference between two kinds of epistemology. I think his epistemology is still starting out from a subjectivist
point of view. Quine describes his epistemology as follows: he says
that he wants to know, on the basis of the data we have available
from the senses, how we build a picture of the world. I think that
is the wrong starting place for epistemology. His concept of data is
purely subjective, and that's why I call him a Cartesian. Quine holds

that the fundamental agreement, that which makes communication possible in the first place, is similarity of nervous reactions. Instead, my epistemology starts from intersubjectivity, that is, from the experience of sharing objectivity. Quine is convinced that I overlook what is epistemologically more meaningful, hence he denies me the status of epistemologist. I think that whatever he attributes to epistemology belongs to biology. There isn't anything you can call perceptive data, evidence, nervous stimulation, until the point when you have thoughts. And thinking presupposes intersubjectivity. This will remain an irreconcilable dispute between Quine and me.

What effect does all this have in relation to the unity of science? It appears that this is also a point of rupture with Quine. . .

Quine believes in the unity of science, like the positivists. I do not. As I said before, there is a difference in the nature of the case between the kind of knowledge we have of other minds, and the kind of knowledge we have of external objects. Many people see this as a way to deny the unity of the sciences.

From this point of view, what kind of knowledge should philosophy concern itself with?

It is up to philosophy to talk about the relations between the three kinds of knowledge, how they differ, and how they interdepend.

But if the sciences of nature investigate the sphere of objectivity, and the human sciences concentrate on knowing other people's minds, what is the science that investigates our own mind? Psychology?

This kind of knowledge is the least interesting because one cannot build much on it. Each one of us knows what he thinks only in the intimacy of his own mind; therefore, I wouldn't call it science.

Where would you place psychoanalysis?

I don't think I would put it anywhere. That psychoanalysis aims to purify and clarify our mind there is no question. Other people can help you be clearer about what you think because we all think things that don't really fit together. However, I don't think that is a special problem of philosophy.

3

Between the New Left and Judaism

Hilary Putnam

"That the work of a philosopher should be reduced to simply thinking about the solution of logical riddles, seems to me to be limiting. But that philosophy should identify with the ambition to save the world seems to me to be too radical." According to Hilary Putnam, the middle ground between the extremes of analytic philosophy and a purely emancipatory impetus resides in a reinterpretation of the realist moment through the screen of pragmatism: in a new version of "pragmatic realism."

Born in Chicago in 1926, and currently teaching at Harvard University, Putnam arrived at this conviction by way of a very tortuous itinerary. His career as a post-analytic thinker, which extends with an encyclopedic range from the philosophy of mind to the philosophy of language, from epistemology to ethics, underwent a phase of profound crisis. During the sixties, concomitant with the pacifist commitment of the American left against the Vietnam War, Putnam threw himself headlong into a political odyssey which saw him serve as the Harvard faculty representative of Students for a Democratic Society and as an active member of a Maoist group, the Progressive Labor Party. Signs of this militancy survive in his interest, very eccentric for a philosopher of his background, in the historical theses of the Frankfurt school, and above all in one of its most recent heirs: Jürgen Habermas.

But that is not all. As for many people, the end of pacifist commitment was not resolved by Putnam in a simple return to the canonized confines of theoretical discipline; instead, it brought to light a mystico-theological awareness tied to the recovery of the Hebrew tradition that, from then onward, Putnam tried to integrate organically into his post-analytic framework.

Apart from the political phase, during which, in his own words, he was never able to "function as a philosopher," Putnam has entrusted the testimony of his complex itinerary to a work of monumental structure and dimension, a sort of *Gesamtwerk* published between 1975 and 1983 as a treatise in three volumes, entitled respectively *Mathematics, Matter, and Method; Mind, Language and Reality;* and *Realism and Reason.* In addition, there are some less weighty volumes, among them his most recent programmatic synthesis, *The Many Faces of Realism* (1987), which comprises the texts of the Paul Carus Lectures, delivered in Washington in 1985.

Putnam's rejection of the strictly analytical horizon of his training is accomplished by the abandonment of the totalizing and deterministic idea of Epistemology-with-a-capital-*E,* or at least of a universal method on the basis of which to decide who is right between two interlocutors, independent of the content of the dispute. Sustained by the formalism of the authors of the Vienna Circle, this new vision of epistemology also lies, according to Putnam, at the origin of that tendency toward exasperated disciplinary professionalization that has ended up by identifying "a constancy with prejudices" as the only cohesion of analytic philosophy.

Only the abandonment of the absolutist epistemological project allows us to divine new and fertile perspectives, derived from the analogy between the epistemological problematics and the ethico-moral ones. For Epistemology-with-a-capital-*E* must be substituted the concept of "moral objectivity," which Putnam formulates in line with the masters of pragmatism, particularly William James. Confronting a series of ethical, historical, and scientific positions, Putnam concludes that in no field is it legitimate to hope for a more ultimate foundation than that of beliefs, and in particular those beliefs that are specific to a particular time and place. The organic ensemble of these beliefs forms a "moral image of the world" that, insofar as it establishes the characteristics of the moral objectivity of that world, can be considered "real" and foundational.

Putnam does not feel alone in reaching these conclusions: from Willard Van Orman Quine's thesis on ontological relativity to Donald Davidson's advanced criticism of the "conceptual scheme–

content" distinction, many post-analytic thinkers have declared their opposition to the traditional dichotomy between the world "in and of itself" and the concepts we use in thinking about and discussing it. The difference is that nobody has wanted to extend this approach, which Putnam defines with the pragmatists as "the point of view of the spectator," to the ethical and moral sphere.

The importance that Putnam confers on moral order, inasmuch as it is pragmatically foundational of the attributes of the reality of the world, is connected to the recovery of the theological horizon of Judaism, from which he carves out for philosophy that salvational impetus the formalistic obsession of analytic thought had made him forget. It is precisely to the biblical tradition that he attributes the formulation of the concepts of "equality among human beings," subsequently secularized and systematized by Immanuel Kant, who in turn inherited it from Jean-Jacques Rousseau, and from the philosophers of the French Revolution. The unique Judaic contribution to Western culture, the ideal of universal equality among men, is one of Putnam's favorite "moral images of the world." Reread through the lenses of some of his guiding authors, among them Søren Kierkegaard, William James, and Ludwig Wittgenstein, this equality assumes two fundamental functions in the sphere of contemporary debate: it is on one hand a bulwark against the nihilism typical of French post-structuralism, and, on the other, an emblem of the emancipatory ideal sustained by that part of German philosophy that includes Habermas and the heirs of the Frankfurt school.

*

Compared with other contemporary American philosophers, you seem to demonstrate more animosity toward analytic thought, even though you were an analytic thinker yourself for a good number of years. How come?

What happened to me, as to many other young American philosophers, was that in graduate school one learned what *not* to like and what not to consider philosophy. We were trained to refute authors and texts. I think that is a terrible thing, and that it should be stopped in all schools, movements and philosophy departments.

It sounds like a kind of censorship. Who were the forbidden authors?

In college I adored Kierkegaard, but I learned that he was considered more of a poet than a philosopher. After him came Marx, in whom I've been interested most of my life. I was a Marxist for a long time, but again I learned to think that Marx is a social theorist and not a philosopher. And I loved Freud, but I learned to think that psychology also was not philosophy. There was a process of narrowing that took place in graduate school, and while I was an assistant professor. I am afraid it was not until I was forty years old that I began to rebel against this habit of thinking of philosophy as being just analytic philosophy.

Analytic philosophy is a vast field, not at all homogeneous, almost half a century old now. I suppose you are referring to the American school of thought?

When I think of my encounter with analytic philosophy, I think of when Herbert Feigl and his collaborators, among them Wilfred Sellars, started putting out anthologies in analytic philosophy. The content of those anthologies determined the philosophical legitimacy of other texts and authors: Gilbert Ryle, John Austin, the logical empiricists, and Bertrand Russell were all analytic philosophers. Even John Dewey was, though it was always a political maneuver to include Dewey, because the analytic philosophers didn't like him very much. Analytic philosophy was created in a certain period, and it has changed a lot since. I would say that if my former self of the 1950s had been put to sleep and awakened today, it would not recognize what is now called analytic philosophy.

You are a very forceful thinker, and therefore in conflict with many contemporary thinkers. But what would the founders of analytic philosophy, like Hans Reichenbach and Rudolf Carnap, think if they were alive today?

When I was teaching at Princeton I worked very closely with Carnap, who was at the Institute for Advanced Studies. I also studied with Reichenbach. Neither man would recognize what we now call analytic philosophy.

On what basis did you detach yourself from the horizon of analytic philosophy?

It was the events of the sixties, a time when I was very active politically. I was faculty advisor for Students for a Democratic Society; I collected draft cards, which was a felony, but I didn't go to jail for it; and I was connected with a Maoist group. I am no longer a Maoist, or even a Marxist, but I think that one of the things I have kept from that period is the idea that philosophy is not, cannot, and should not be simply an academic discipline. I think I owe this to the sixties, which was in many ways a transformative period in my life.

Don't you think that the idea of philosophy as a global discipline, a socially, ethically, and aesthetically engaged discipline, is a typically Continental characteristic?

I think the term *Continental philosophy* is no longer a good one, because national differences have reappeared. The difference now between German philosophy and French philosophy is so great that to use the term *Continental philosophy* is no longer useful. Italian philosophy has a somewhat different character. Italian philosophy looks around a lot, so does German philosophy. I think the German philosophers read both French and analytic philosophy, which is a very good thing, whereas the French philosophers still think that you only need to read French.

You are saying in essence that in Europe there exist two great traditions, the French and the German. What is the basis of their profound irreconcilability?

I think that German philosophy, ever since German idealism, has retained the idea of philosophy as redemptive. Habermas, in his book *Knowledge and Human Interest,* holds as a philosophical keystone the notion of a "redemptive interest" of the human being, an interest in some kind of salvation, either personal or social, or both. I think that almost every German philosopher has seen philosophy as having some kind of salvific mission, a notion that continues to inform the character of German philosophy. I think that French philosophy is different. Since the French turned away from existentialism, French philosophers have been dominated by a view of politics that I very much dislike: the politics of tearing everything down in the hope that maybe something good will appear. It was this sort of policy that brought Hitler to power in Germany, so I'm really quite glad French philosophers don't have more political influence than they do.

Are you referring to deconstruction and postmodernism?

I'm referring to those who think that our culture is so terribly repressive that it should be destroyed, in the hope that from its ruins something better will appear. Also, a certain playacting, a certain theatricality seems to have become a must in French culture in the last few years. Jacques Bouveresse, who was himself very critical of the dominant current in French philosophy, once said that French philosophers have perfected the art of sounding very radical without saying anything that will keep them out of the next socialist government.

In these two traditions, the French and German, who are the leaders, who is "making" the history of philosophy?

I think that Jürgen Habermas is the greatest contemporary representative of German philosophy, perhaps the greatest philosopher on the Continent. The greatest contemporary representative of French philosophy, although the French themselves don't rate him as highly as the Americans do, is Jacques Derrida. I think that the difference in the vital impetus of Habermas and Derrida is enormous. From Derrida one can learn something valuable about reading texts. However, when one tries to read every text as though the point were to see how it deconstructed itself, that also becomes a false way of reading. Only a few texts should be read deconstructively. Starting with his early book, *Speech and Phenomenon,* Derrida proposes a systematic method that rests on a philosophy of language that is very weak.

From the linguistic point of view, the main point of reference for Derrida remains Ferdinand de Saussure.

That's true. Although I think that Saussure was a genius in many ways, his philosophy of language doesn't really work. There is a constant contradiction in Saussure, which he recognized himself, on the issue of indeterminacy: the possibility or impossibility of translation and hermeneutics. Saussure's view implies that every language is hermetically sealed from every other, that every language has its own world, and that no translation is possible. I think that Derrida's notions rest on Saussure and his proto-structuralist view in that peculiar way French thinkers have of resting on previous French thinkers. Post-structuralists are nothing but neo-structuralists.

Going back to the question of the "vital impetus," in what sense is Habermas a better teacher than Derrida?

Habermas seems to me a broader thinker, a "God-thinker." He's not just thinking about language and about how language destroys itself. Habermas is trying to think about how the parts of our culture hang together, about what's wrong with our culture, and what might be done to make it better. And he's trying to do this with some kind of very large vision, perhaps the largest vision since Karl Marx: the attempts to see how social theory, epistemology, and the theory of language all fit together.

How did your approach to Habermas come about, directly or through the Frankfurt school?

Directly, but I am convinced that his relationship to the Frankfurt school is inescapable. Not only does he teach in Frankfurt, but he has a reverence for what happened at Frankfurt in the past, for Theodor Adorno and Walter Benjamin in particular. He and Karl Otto Apel really constitute a new development in German thought. In fact, it is interesting to compare the developments in what I call the New Frankfurt school with the American pragmatism of William James and Charles Peirce.

But in the New Frankfurt school there is a whole political and emancipative project that is difficult to find in the metaphysical and pluralist thrust of James, or in Peirce's semiotics. This seems to me to be clear even in the neo-pragmatist perspective of Richard Rorty.

I think American pragmatism felt that democracy was not just a Western phenomenon, as we say nowadays. Some people criticize anyone who thinks that third world countries should be democratic, because they assume that it is an attempt to impose the culture of the West. It would not be so if they saw democracy, or an aspect of democracy, to be connected with a modern view of truth. What I mean by a modern view of truth is not just a postmedieval view, but a view that comes at the end of the nineteenth century when one begins to see that even the physics of Newton and Galileo are not able to provide certainty. Peirce himself said that if he had to name his philosophy he would have called it "fallibilism," the idea that all truth worthy of the name is uncertain and subject to correction.

Isn't this "fallibilist" perspective of negating any totalizing, universal, or metahistorical truth similar to that of poststructuralism and French deconstruction?

Yes, in a certain way. But the French take it as meaning that there is no such thing as truth. In fact, in conversation Derrida is much more reasonable: he would say that the notion of truth is contradictory, but that it is absolutely indispensable. I wish he would stress this side more in his writing. Peirce once used a wonderful metaphor, the first really anti-foundationalist metaphor I know of. He said that it's as if we were walking on unfirm ground, on swampy ground, and that that was good because, if the ground were firm, there would be no reason to go anywhere. In the manifesto of pragmatism, *How to Make Our Ideas Clear,* he basically gives an account of truth in terms of a Hegelian sequence. You would first believe in what he calls the "method of authority," and truth is what the authorities say it is. When you began to see that you could no longer do that, that the pope and the king were sometimes wrong, you'd go to what he calls the "method agreeable to reason," which is the method of metaphysics and of classical rationalism. And he feels that, today, both of these methods have been overcome, *aufgehoben,* although there are plenty of people in the world who talk as if they were still valid.

Rorty was the first to raise the possibility of a post- or neo-pragmatist development in contemporary thought. Why have you never fully taken part in the elaboration of such a perspective?

Rorty attributes to truth an emotional role: he uses the notion of truth to pay someone a compliment. I do not agree with him; I don't see the pragmatists as he does. I think that Peirce was saying that the only third way is to recognize that while truth is uncertain, any truth worthy of the name has to be subject to tests and subject to public discussion. And this, of course, is a theme with the New Frankfurt school. Apel wrote a book on Peirce, pointing out both the connection between his and Wittgenstein's argument on private language, on the one hand, and the deep meditation on the idea of an ideal speech situation by Habermas, on the other. But I think the key idea, which Dewey makes very explicit, is that if we assume that there is such a thing as truth in ethics or truth in politics, then it must be subject to the same constraints as scientific truth. That is to say, we must test it and retest it and allow others to test it. And we must constantly discuss the methods of verification. William James used to say that there was no one method for finding truth, not even making predictions or sensory experience. We have to keep having experience and keep discussing it, we have to keep on talking and keep on experiencing. The ethic of democracy, that it is our right to test our political ideas, stops short of denying others the same right. This is connected with a postmodern notion of truth, and it seems to me to be the common element of pragmatism and the New Frankfurt school, one I find very attractive.

The relationship between French post-structuralism and the New Frankfurt school has already been marked by an open confrontation between Habermas and Jean-François Lyotard, a very intensive *querelle,* that Rorty tried to resolve with a notion of truth that is both postmodern and socially conscious.

The problem, as the pragmatists are well aware, is that while we have agreement in science—or rather, in some sciences, because the younger sciences do not have as much agreement, as we see in physics—as to how to test things, we don't have that degree of agreement in politics or in ethics. Our disagreements are not just over a particular program or principle but over how programs and principles are to be tested. Two things are needed. First of all, one has to give up the idea of trying to speak from a God's-eye view, including the attempt to say from a God's-eye view that there is no God's-eye view. Second, one can only criticize or discuss ethical or political programs if one is committed to advancing what Habermas calls the "redemptive interest." And for that, as William James says, you have to listen to the cries of the wounded. A very simple, short sentence.

However, the problem remains in the mediation between these two terms: the abandonment of the divine view and the necessity of a salvific interest. And if this mediation cannot be anything but contextual, in what sense can there exist metahistorical values, or principles, like democracy, that transcend ethnicity?

I want to stress that I don't think democracy is just a Western phenomenon. One problem with the view that democracy is just an ethnic thing, or that socialism is just an ethnic thing, is that this doesn't account for the enthusiasm with which people in the third world responded, starting in the last century, to whatever they heard, however imperfectly, about both democracy and socialism. We shouldn't abandon the ideals, but we should criticize the hypocrisy with which the West talks about these ideals, and the contrast between the rhetoric of the West and the practice of the West. I think part of the real tragedy of socialism in the twentieth century is that it has become anti-democratic. It suffices to think about Stalinism.

Democracy, then, is a value.

I hold democracy to be a value, not just an ethical value, but a cognitive value in every area. Democracy is a requirement for experimental inquiry in any area. To reject democracy is to reject the idea of being experimental. I think we have had enough experience to know what happens when we say we don't need to be experimental.

Among the post-analytic philosophers, you are probably the only one to have developed a strong theological interest, oriented toward the recuperation of the Hebrew tradition. How is it that someone like you, with a logician's background, has at a certain point rehabilitated the centrality of God, of mysticism, and of the interpretation of the sacred text?

I think that what makes one religious is one's inner experience. It doesn't make sense to convert others. Being religious is compatible with skepticism about revelation. In the Jewish or the Christian traditions, which are inspired and holy, there is something I just can't explain. That doesn't mean that they are not also human products; in the eighteenth century humanity was shocked when it read the Bible for the first time as a human product, but the Bible is not a blueprint for a perfect society. For example, the society the Jews are told to have is a far juster society than the ones they saw around them in Egypt and Babylon, or even in Greece and Rome. They are told, for example, to treat their slaves much better than people around them were treating their slaves, but they weren't told not to have slaves. There are some things that are said which I regard as plain wrong, the prejudice against homosexuals, for example. The sense of the sacred is not necessarily a good thing; it can lead one to do terrible things. Of course for that very reason in the nineteenth century people said we should stop believing in the sacred, and then we won't do terrible things any more. Then we had two very atheist dictators, called Stalin and Hitler, who between them killed even more people than anyone had killed in the name of the sacred.

Then, it is not simply about religion. Your Judaism is something different. . .

For me the word "religion" is a bad word. I would say that my Judaism represents a sense of limits. Jewish thinkers often quote a passage from the Talmud, and it's almost a cliché to quote it, but I still like to do it: it says that it's not up to us to finish the task, but neither are we free not to take it up. For me religion means a sense of human limits. The problem with humanism, as developed by Feuerbach, is that it meant the deification of man, and I don't see anything in this century that makes me want to deify man. Like Ben Schwartz, I think that man is the worst god there is.

Do you share this recovery of the Hebrew tradition with other American intellectuals, such as the literary theorist Harold Bloom?

It seems to me that Bloom has another religion, the religion of art. It seems to me an awfully patronizing view, because what he implies is that spiritual life is for novelists and critics and that all the rest of us can do is read wonderful books. The message is that writing is the successor to religion.

How do you look at the work of a "philosopher of writing" such as Emmanuel Levinas?

His knowledge and understanding of Jewish religion is very deep.

Is there or isn't there a spirit of the time in your mystical thrust?

No, I don't think so. I believe that if I had been Greek, I would have been Greek orthodox. I think that one way or another, there is something deep within me which demands that sort of expression.

How do you thematize the specific sense of universality and transcendence of the present in Judaism, compared to other religions?

Every time Judaism has been universalized, it has been bad for the Jews. I think the particularity of Judaism, and one of the things I like about it, is that we are not a religion which says that everyone has to become a Jew.

One could say, then, that you have a "pluralistic" view of Judaism?

The notion of pluralism remains crucial in our time. It is anchored in pragmatism, more in Dewey than in James or Peirce. Thanks to irreversible technological advancement, and the great mobility of people, it is clear that the world is not going to break into hermetically sealed groups. In contemporary society pluralism means preserving difference while preserving communication.

Let's return to philosophy. You have written that philosophy is neither an art nor a science, but a third modality.

Philosophy is as fundamental as art or science. For a long time, it was assimilated by religion. Today, Derrida on one side and the analytic philosophers on the other, are trying to assimilate this unique modality either to art or to science. Analytic philosophers basically see philosophy as a science, only less developed, vaguer and newer, while Derrida basically sees philosophy as literature, as art. I don't think either is correct. Philosophy can neither become pure writing nor a matter of proofs. Naturally, there is room for arguments in philosophy, but it is not simply a question of arguments.

In this third modality of philosophy you identify the sphere of the ordinary, or the everyday. Is this tied to Wittgenstein and, if so, in what way?

I don't think that ordinary and everyday are synonyms. *Everyday* has a bad connotation, and *ordinary* has a good connotation. This is very hard for me, partly because I am still struggling with it, struggling with the right way of formulating it in my own work and my own writing. About Wittgenstein: I have thought more about him than any other philosopher. He does not have a proper "theory" of language, or of language games. So you can read Wittgenstein as a sort of minor Austin, but I don't think that's what Wittgenstein is about. There are at least two other ways of reading Wittgenstein. The first is that one can read Wittgenstein as simply a voice of despair, a voice saying that philosophy is over. The second way is much more tentative and much more difficult, but I feel it's what I would like to do and it's what I think Stanley Cavell is doing. That is to say that Wittgenstein wants to shut down or disabuse us, or better yet, to disabuse something which has been called philosophy, in order to make room for something else, something that is very hard to characterize.

How do you characterize this "something else" which is philosophy?

I associate it with what Heidegger called *Denken*. Cavell uses the term "ordinary." Some people associate it with ethics. Kant said that he tried to limit science to make room for faith. I remain convinced that most people, under a certain layer of postmodern sophistication, still believe that some things are absolutely wrong. Ordinary does not mean going to the post office and mailing a letter, it means faith that the way we think and live isn't all a fiction or an illusion, that the illusion is rather all these tremendous intellectual constructions that make the way we think and live look like an illusion. This is what Wittgenstein was trying to make room for. Just as Marx turned Hegel's world upside down, today Wittgenstein would think that the philosophers and the literary theorists have the world upside down.

Wittgenstein, then, has been your teacher?

I'm not sure I would define him as my teacher. If I had studied with him, I don't know that I would have developed an independent style of philosophy.

Concerning the real world, the world of illusion, and about looking at the world backwards: have you ever been interested in psychoanalysis?

I think that psychoanalysis is a way of seeing. Freud is telling us that there is an infant in every one of us. An emotional infant, which is another way of saying an emotional cripple, because an infant isn't really suited to live an adult life. Many of us are two-year-olds trying to deal with the responsibilities of thirty- and forty- and fifty- and sixty-year-olds, which is a terrible way to go through life. I think Freud tried, as Marx tried, to make his discoveries a closed system of ideas. I don't believe in closed systems of ideas, but that is not to say that one cannot learn from Marx and Freud. When psychoanalysis works, it becomes something that doesn't end when you leave the therapy. It becomes something you do for yourself.

Don't you think that art could also be seen as a technique of observation and self-observation?

I never made up my mind about how much of a unity the arts are. Is art a unitary concept? Of any aesthetic writing, one can intuit the art it refers to. For example, with Kant it was clearly painting. And also that of Nelson Goodman, whom I admire very much.

Putting together all your definitions of what philosophy is, it seems one can conclude that it represents for you a great, encyclopedic adventure of mental practices.

I think that there is a unity to philosophy, even though it has different aspects, both disciplinary and geographic. The Germans, as I mentioned earlier, emphasize the salvific aspect. Then there is a scientific aspect, which analytic philosophers emphasize, a literary aspect, and so on. But these are, I think, aspects of one thing. I think that when one tries to cut philosophy up, to isolate one of these aspects in the way that analytic philosophy has tried to do with the scientific aspect, then philosophy behaves like a neurotic individual. And you get all the typical symptoms of neurosis: fantasy and compulsion, repetition, and, finally, the return of the repressed.

Perhaps you experience your past as an analytic philosopher as the return of the repressed. . .

I believe that analytic philosophy started with respect for argument. The problem is that after awhile all philosophy had to be argument, and people didn't know what to argue about. Therefore, imaginary objects emerged: possible worlds are just as real as imaginary ones. That seems to me a beautiful example of the return of the repressed. The analytic movement started out as an anti-metaphysical movement, but today, it is fair to say that it is the most metaphysical movement of all. The proof is that the masters of analytic philosophy keep speaking about "intuition."

It is almost ironic that only now, at the end of our conversation, the issue of metaphysics should arise.

I don't criticize analytic philosophy for being metaphysical, I am not an anti-metaphysics militant. My problem with analytic philosophy is that it is empty. All philosophy does not have to be argument, and all arguments do not have to be in the analytic style. Kierkegaard, for example, does have arguments, even though analytic philosophers will never recognize it. It is the same with Wittgenstein: his arguments often have a pedagogical character, the objective of which is not to explain something to the reader, but to get the reader to work things out by himself. This, I think, is the true purpose of philosophy.

4

Anarchy at Harvard

Robert Nozick

The publication of *Anarchy, State, and Utopia* in 1974 gave a new thrust of hope and optimism to America, shaken by the Watergate scandal and inevitably on its way to the first international defeat in its history, marked by the retreat of the troops from Vietnam. Its author, Robert Nozick, had nothing in common with either the image of the Great Old European in the style of Herbert Marcuse, tutelar deity of sixties liberalism, or that of the strict professor in the style of John Rawls, the teacher of neo-contractualism, who had just published his most important essay, *A Theory of Justice* (1971), still considered a landmark of American and European political philosophy.

Nozick was born in Brooklyn in 1938 to a family of Russian Jews. He was a young man who, with a studied candor, juxtaposed an extremely strict philosophical training, constructed layer by layer on the rigors of analytical thought, with the recovery of an individualistic anarchical tradition that, in American culture, had its founding father in Henry David Thoreau.

Unlike his Harvard colleague Stanley Cavell, who in the same years revived the long-dormant tradition of Thoreau and transcendentalism in a "genealogical" key, Nozick was making it for the first time a programmatic discourse. Against the line of French utopianism in the style of Charles Fourier, centered on the concept of an "ideal community," Nozick proposed a pluralistic anarchism, based on the coexistence of different social events in a potentially peaceful conversation with one another.

The operative horizon of Nozick's thought, however, does not exhaust itself in a social and political program so much as—and this is his most fascinating aspect—it is reflected at different levels within the philosophical fabric. The critique of the "coercive" essence of philosophical "argumentation" and the consequent prefiguration of a libertarian alternative are in fact the real fulcrum of Nozick's reflection. Initially laid out in *Anarchy, State, and Utopia*, this problematic receives a more explicit formulation in *Philosophical Explanations*, published in 1981.

The ethical interest that led Nozick to philosophy, in a New York City climate attentive to progressive ferments, was as crucial to his becoming a political thinker as was his affiliation with the analytic philosophers. Among them, he preferred above all Carl Hempel, one of the neo-positivist Viennese émigrés who, from the citadel of Princeton University, was his teacher and guide before and after the completion of his doctoral dissertation.

It was from Hempel that Nozick learned the notion of "scientific explanation" which, in a "libertarian" epistemological reelaboration, represents the key to change in his thought, ultimately interpretable as a radical alternative to analytic philosophy.

The objective of *Philosophical Explanations* is the reexamination of the "Kantian form" of some fundamental theoretical questions; or, in other words, an inquiry into the conditions of possibility of problematics such as the objectivity of ethical truth, or the roots of knowledge. According to Nozick, such analysis must be conducted in an alternative form to the classical one of argument, which, brought to its apogee by the logical technicalities of analytic philosophy, is based on a fundamental compulsion of the reader to believe, to convince himself of fixed consequences, when given certain premises and presented with a "proof." The repressiveness implicit in the practice of argument is suggested, among other things, by its root meaning, which in English refers to a disagreement, a violent quarrel between contrasting opinions.

In contrast to the coercive power of argument, Nozick proposes the concept of *explanation*, which, rather than forcing the reader to make specific conclusions, would "stimulate" him to alternative ways of thinking. Tearing the philosophical enterprise away from the spirit of dispute and returning it to a new, more pluralistic basis of comprehension is Nozick's central objective. He was the first to try to bring the emancipatory premises of democratic utopia into the confines of analyticism.

The philosophical aim of "explanation" is not exhausted in the purely epistemological satisfaction of the proof; it extends itself to the ethical horizon of moral improvement. The motivations that move a reader to belief are curiosity and a desire to deepen his or her comprehension of the world: or, at least, of the dimensions of introspection and moral growth that makes of philosophy an "expressive" discipline.

In opposition to the "Puritans of the mind"—the deities of empiricism, tied to the factual sobriety of phenomena and to the systematic limitation of the themes of analysis—Nozick has developed since the mid-sixties a profound interest in the oriental philosophies, particularly Indian. The expressivity of philosophy, even when viewed through this lens, is therefore not identifiable with the conflictuality of a European-style existential excavation, but rather with the meditative necessity of a more global and fundamental outlook on the great speculative issues.

Nozick dedicated his last book, which is certainly very literary in its concept of philosophy, to the extension of this project. The book, published in 1989 and entitled *The Examined Life,* is a memoir of philosophical explanations. Here, the notion of explanation is understood in an "applicative" key, in the sense that it enters into the merits of some "fundamental questions" of philosophy, understood as a dynamic adventure in the transformations of the self. Among these questions are death, selflessness, and happiness.

*

Let's begin with the most recent chapter in your itinerary, *The Examined Life,* **which has so different a structure from your preceding work as to resemble the testament of a moralist. In the introduction you mention the importance of philosophy remaining tied to those "fundamental questions" of existence, defined in your** *Philosophical Explanations,* **in three nuclei: the objectivity of truth, self-identity, and the limits of knowledge.**

I don't know if I saw *The Examined Life* as seeking explanations in quite the same way that I set up philosophy in *Philosophical*

Explanations. In *Philosophical Explanations* I wanted to analyze the Kantian form of some fundamental philosophical questions: How are certain things possible? How is knowledge possible? How are objective ethical truths possible? I wanted to set about providing possible answers to those questions. In *The Examined Life* I didn't have the same sharp questions in mind about possibilities in things. I mean, how can free will be possible given causal determinism? How can knowledge be possible given skeptical arguments? You cannot think about life stopping at its conditions of possibility. I just wanted to probe more deeply into what made life meaningful and valuable.

One could almost speak of an "existential turn."

It would be too narcissistic, although it's true that the last chapter of *Philosophical Explanations* is entitled "Philosophy and the Meaning of Life." If I had to define my work in the last few years, I would say that it has a more personal voice and tone about the reflection of a number of "fundamental questions."

Running through the table of contents of your last book, one has the impression of looking at more of a literary than a philosophical text, due to the structure and the style. The chapters have titles referring to dying, parents and children, sexuality and love. Why has a pure philosopher such as yourself opted for this "existential" adventure of writing?

From my training in philosophy I have learned to make distinctions and to think things through rigorously. You may wonder what someone like that, a mind trained like that, has to say about the questions of life, the topics of life, including love and sexuality, the topics that actually concern not only philosophers, but most other people in the world. It was an experiment to see whether the kind of training that I had could be brought to bear on less sharp questions, on fuzzier issues, that are of deep human concern.

One could say that you tried to sort out the significance of your philosophical training.

It wasn't just to see whether that training could be brought to bear on life, or to test the dynamics of philosophical reflection *tout court*. At the beginning of *The Examined Life*, I tried to respond to these questions, writing from my whole being to the whole being of the reader, and I think there was a dissatisfaction that I had been feeling with the way one treats those questions in philosophical writing: that it is the rational mind speaking to the rational mind of the reader. With this last book, I wanted to throw myself fully into writing, not only with my reason, but with whatever else I could bring to bear on it. I keep looking at it as something different from my typical creatures, such as *Philosophical Explanations*.

At the heart of *Philosophical Explanations* is your criticism of the "coercive power" of argumentation. The whole notion of *explanation* is formulated in an alternative key to precisely the repressive potential of classical logic. From this perspective, *The Examined Life* seems the necessary consequence of *Philosophical Explanations*—a kind of literary celebration, presented as an alternative to the Western concept of argumentation.

The Examined Life was conceived as a noncoercive book, even less coercive than *Philosophical Explanations*, where I was presenting one person's thoughts in the hope that it would stimulate alternative thoughts in other people. I wasn't asking the readers to accept what I was writing as the truth about these topics, but as a vehicle that could help them to think more deeply about those questions.

How did the idea that philosophical argumentation expresses a coercive potential originate? Is it that you identify the concept of argumentation with the formalistic emphasis you have attributed to Anglo-American analytic tradition?

I was always taught that truth had to construct arguments or proofs that couldn't be avoided. The language of analytic philosophy "forces" the reader to a conclusion through a knock-down argument. Young people and children think that an argument involves people with raised voices, yelling at each other in interpersonal, negative interaction. Then we learn in philosophy that an argument is something else, a sequence of steps that gets you from premises to the conclusion. But why do we actually call the sequence of steps that gets you from premises to conclusion an argument? I don't know whether it's the same way in other languages, and whether "yelling" has the same emotional overtones it has in English. It would be interesting to investigate, in the history of philosophy, how what philosophers construct came to be called arguments. I believe that at the root of this is the desire to make somebody believe something.

In your first book, Anarchy, State, and Utopia, you still hadn't achieved this sort of Copernican revolution, and it seems to me that you present precisely a series of arguments to sustain your thesis, even if you do so in an unusual way.

In *Philosophical Explanations* I began to understand that I wasn't satisfying the impulse that had brought me to philosophy: I never wanted to force people to believe things, I wanted to help them understand things better. Therefore, I thought that it would be better to structure the enterprise of philosophy around the activity of understanding, rather than interpersonal activity of argument, which didn't fit my motivation for coming to philosophy. I believe that even though many philosophical dilemmas are formulated according to this coercive logic, a distortion takes place.

In your own intellectual history, when did the need to free yourself from coercive argumentation arise?

In 1974, when I published *Anarchy, State, and Utopia*, everybody recognized in this book a "libertarian political philosophy." It was very anti-coercive in the political realm. Perhaps there was a natural outgrowth in continuity, and I came to be anti-coercive in the philosophical realm also. *Philosophical Explanations* came out in 1981, though I had completed it in 1979, and if I were to date my "anti-coercive illuminations," I would say that it was sometime between 1974 and 1979. I suppose that academic practice has also stimulated my interest in formulating a theoretically more libertarian thinking: when visitors are invited to read papers in university settings, it consists of somebody coming to read an argument essentially to convince the audience of certain views. The audience fights against that, raising objections. Why does this battle take place? Why isn't there a more cooperative way to carry on these activities?

Don't you think that the social and cultural atmosphere in the sixties and seventies contributed in some way to the consolidation of your positions?

It may be that some of the themes of the students in the sixties had an influence on me. For example, the notion of domination, as it was understood by the students in the sixties in relation to institutions, has made me alert to the repressive potential inherent in the intellectual realm.

In those years, was Michel Foucault an important point of reference?

No. Not then. In fact, at that point I hadn't read Foucault. It was really only after *Philosophical Explanations* that I read Foucault on sexuality and on issues about power.

In a certain sense, one could almost establish a parallel between Foucault's discourse on the unveiling of repressive power implicit in the institutional and linguistic structures that form our culture, and your criticism of the coercive potential or philosophical argumentation.

Yes. I hadn't seen that connection, and it certainly hadn't been the genesis of my books, for, at the time, I had not read Foucault at all. However, I recognize that his thoughts, not only on language, but on how intellectual subjects get organized for coercive purposes, especially in *The Archeology of Knowledge,* would fit and connect with this theme.

In the absence of teachers, how did your passage from analytic philosophy to political thought take place?

Even if *Anarchy, State, and Utopia* represented radical political views, the philosophical tools that I used there were still the same ones I used when I thought about philosophy of science and epistemology. I had actually started out as a young person quite interested in issues of social and political philosophy, and then got drawn off into the philosophy of science while, in the late fifties, I was an undergraduate at Columbia, where many of the best teachers were working in the philosophy of science. I got drawn into questions about scientific explanations, inductive logic, and support of scientific theories. I then went to Princeton as a graduate student where Hempel was a central figure. It was then that I decided to write my dissertation on the philosophy of science and specifically on confirmation theory, a theory of the theories of support for scientific hypotheses, which helped to accept or reject the scientific hypothesis.

Then, Carl Hempel was a true teacher for you?

He gave me wonderful suggestions about how to pursue my work. Once the dissertation was over I became involved in decision theory, that is, theories trying to define the notion of rational choice when it comes to accepting or rejecting a scientific hypothesis. Those theories had been developed mainly by statisticians and economists, who problematized how you can rationally make a choice when you don't know for sure what the consequences of the action available to you will be. A central issue was the use of mathematical parameters and the notion of probability.

And when did your interest in fundamental questions arise?

I finished my doctoral dissertation when I was very young, at about the age of twenty-three. I thought that I wanted to direct my philosophical work to questions that I really cared to answer. This is going to sound strange because one assumes that one will work on things that one cares to answer, but there are a lot of intellectually intriguing questions in philosophy: puzzles, paradoxes, little things that one can think about, especially in the Anglo-American analytic tradition, which were there for their own sake. I had a little imaginary experiment I haven't thought about since then: if I were working on certain topics for two years, and if I were in an automobile accident that caused me to be in a coma, and then, when I came out of the coma, was told that somebody had solved this problem, but that it had been done in such a difficult way that I would have to spend a year of my life trying to understand the solution, would I still be interested in it? This way of reasoning is paradoxical, but the question is still there: why?

Do you think that the typically analytic devotion to this "formalistic" idea of philosophy, unhampered by any application or interdisciplinary perspective, is still shared by many people?

During my course of studies, there certainly was a great emphasis on philosophy for philosophy's sake, as in art for art's sake, and therefore in technical facility. I was never really attracted by it.

From very early on, my way of thinking became more "personal," even though I didn't formalize this position until much later.

Your "divorce" from analytic thought must have caused conflicts with teachers, colleagues, and students with orthodox positions.

I'm sure that as a graduate student I thought of myself as an analytic philosopher, but it was never a movement that I especially wanted to belong to. I just wanted to think about questions, and here were tools that I could use in thinking about them. I always thought that analytic philosophy wasn't large enough to contain everything I wanted to say. I wanted to be a philosopher who drew on analytic philosophy, and anything else that would be helpful in advancing understanding. However, regarding tension with other philosophers. . . Well, you might have to ask the other philosophers.

Actually, I am referring to the sensation of moving along the margins of a discipline, of being almost an outsider.

With my last book, *The Examined Life,* I wasn't thinking only about philosophy, so there was a sense of marginalization. Perhaps now I have some feeling that I need to do another book at the center of philosophical work, a little less experimental. You have been referring only to my published material, but teaching has always been very important to me. While I was writing *Philosophical Explanations,* and also years before, when I was writing *Anarchy, State, and Utopia,* many of my courses were centered on Indian philosophy, classical as well as contemporary.

What were the stages by which you fell in love with the "other" philosophies, Indian and, more generally, oriental? Was it in the seventies, again in tune with the times?

The Indian philosophical tradition contains very abstract reasoning, but it also tries to come to terms with certain unusual experiences that some of these Indian thinkers have had, either by doing yoga practice, or meditation. I recall when, in the sixties, in the United States, books on Indian philosophy were popping up in the philosophy sections of bookstores, and I recall wondering why these books were there, since I was familiar with the section of the bookstore on European and Anglo-American analytic philosophy. There were students in the sixties who experimented with drugs of various sorts and were having experiences that those books fit most closely. At some point, I began to take these writings in Indian philosophy seriously, and that is how it became one of the central intellectual topics in my work. And I had been raised in an empiricist tradition that said to take your experiences seriously.

Wasn't there an "existential crisis" when, thanks to the meeting with the Orient, you came to understand that the radius of experiences is wider and more opaque then the empiricist tradition presumed?

I wanted to think about what a philosophy that took into account other branches of experiences, such as the mystical or religious, might look like. Then, I became interested in those theories for their own sake. They were vast metaphysical structures of an unusual sort.

I find that your very deep interest in Indian thought could be a key to changing the interpretation of your more recent work. It seems to me that, in sequence, your last two books reveal a fascination with the notion of "presence," in the sense that pure meditation on the pluralistic character of reality becomes central.

I find the notion of presence very congenial. I took meditative experience seriously in *The Examined Life,* and I also took seriously unusual ways of looking at present experience, and what it may signify and reveal.

By "presence" I refer to the search for a totality, an all-encompassing notion of Being. Hasn't the Orient suggested something about this?

The Orient represented an openness of mind I didn't know before, the necessity to direct my attention to more global, inclusive, and fundamental questions.

How have you reconciled your Jewish background, in which totality is always the product of a dialectic, with the spherical "pan-vision" proposed by Indian metaphysics?

I became aware of my Jewish background only when my children

were born. I hadn't thought about it for fifteen years. From a philosophical point of view, I feel that the day I can embrace the hermeneutic tradition is still very far away. Jewish philosophy is impreg-
nated with "historical visions" and forbids every form of originality.
On the contrary, I have always started again from zero.

About your relationship with history, I am reminded of a metaphor about knowledge I found in *Philosophical Explanations*. It is
about the Parthenon, the archetype of aesthetic classical knowledge, which, you say, keeps its beauty beyond time and physical
decomposition. To the image of the Parthenon you oppose another type of knowledge, which follows the model of a very high
and thin tower, composed of bricks placed one on top of another. Opposed to the Parthenon, which in the form of ruin
keeps its charm, the tower could not withstand any mutilation.

Philosophers tried to deduce a global vision of reality from a few
basic principles. A brick is placed upon another until a huge philosophical tower is built. The risk is that if the brick on the bottom
is removed, everything falls apart, taking along those insights that
proliferated independently from the very beginning. While writing
The Examined Life, I stayed home for a year and I realized, for the
first time, that the stratified beauty of a city is the highest achievement. It is particularly meaningful that I should say that, since I
grew up in Brooklyn.

To remain on the subject of classical iconology, your feeling
about history could then be described as a sort of Janus figure:
on one side you propose the instance of "beginning from zero,"
and on the other you are fascinated by the "archeological," the
harmonious survival, the ineluctable reemergence of the meanings of the past in the present.

My great master was Socrates; I don't have another sense of history.

And why not a great American, like Ralph Waldo Emerson, who
also has theorized about the value of originality, and who, like
you, experienced the fascination of Oriental reflection on the absolute?

Although Emerson and Thoreau are Americans, in this country we
don't have a tendency to pursue things in the line of tradition. My

mother was born here, but her parents came from Russia, and my father came from Russia at the age of sixteen.

Why do you use the term anarchy? What does it mean?

I think that there are two different anarchist traditions. The first is the anarchists of the left, whose predecessor is Charles Fourier: their guideline is the notion of the ideal community. The second type is the individualist anarchist, and its first representatives were Henry D. Thoreau and Mikhail Bakunin. I feel closer to this second line, because it defends a plurality of ideals instead of the myth of an ideal community. It allows us to save values such as private property and personal initiative.

Your thought could be seen, and has been interpreted, as an apotheosis of pluralism. Do you agree?

I think the concept of pluralism is articulated by two different categories: time, which translates pluralism in terms of pragmatism; and space, in which pluralism encourages the coexistence of different entities. I believe that in America, Nelson Goodman developed the second notion of pluralism. I personally believe in a combination of the two alternatives—the possibility of diverse unities of thought coexisting, projecting different perspectives on the same reality.

Do you believe that your philosophical vision of pluralism could enter into a dialogue with other spheres of the contemporary debate, such as neo-pragmatism or the discussion on the nature of liberalism?

Whereas I see my last book, *The Examined Life,* as an adventure within the transforming self, in the sense that it doesn't dig or excavate, but only describes the developments and metamorphoses of the soul, my next book will involve me with debates about the rationality of science, in the sense meant by Kuhn, and with the questions raised by Rorty about philosophy's special authority to set up norms. If philosophy is not the foundation for everything else, in what way is philosophy the judge of other intellectual activities, and what does it have to contribute to other intellectual activities? About liberalism, I have the feeling that this debate about the roots of rationality will involve me with the nature of social science. By rationality I don't mean only rational thought, but rational action, and the ways in which theories of rational action will play a role in the social sciences, sociology, and historical explanations. It may be that I will discover that I have something more to say about liberalism and political thought. I have ideas about my next project and about possible things afterwards, but where one goes after the next project depends on what the content of the next project turns out to be.

Couldn't it be that after the book on rationality, which you have decided *a priori* will be more technical, more strictly philosophical than the last one, you will come to understand that it is no longer the time to write in philosophical "technical terms," and you will decide to continue in the mode of moralistic reminiscence, à la Montaigne, which you have touched upon in *The Examined Life*?

I like my intellectual itinerary to be open-ended. I'm aware that I'm paying a price for this, but it is consistent with my temperament: I pick up suggestions and images while I am already on the way.

As you speak, I'm reminded of a work by Borges, the story of a painter who in his entire life doesn't understand the subject of his paintings. He paints and paints without stopping. Then one day, just before dying, he looks at all his paintings and notices that he had progressively been painting his own portrait.

In *The Examined Life* there is a section about creativity in which I write that one's work, even when it doesn't appear to be that way, is often very personal. A personal transformation takes place, and part of modifying concepts, not only in artistic work but in intellectual work as well, corresponds to certain alterations in one's own self, hence creating a new portrait, as in Borges's story. I'm convinced that if I hadn't written one line of what I wrote in my last three books, I would have missed something.

Is that how you feel about *The Examined Life*?

In some way I feel uneasy about this book, because in American philosophy people write with a very different object in mind. When I get that feeling, I read thirty or forty pages of it, and then I am glad that I wrote this book. There are different aspects of one's full being and one's mental range, and one wants to express and develop them in one's work. In this sense, philosophy differs from technical scientific work. I don't know if Quine and Davidson feel this impulse—they may consider me indulgent, and probably think that philosophy should not be as expressive as I think. But I would be unhappy in a mode of work that wasn't in some way personally expressive.

Your idea that philosophy must be able to "express" the movements of the soul detaches it from science and draws it closer to literature. In this sense, philosophy loses its epistemological privilege and transforms itself into a genre of "writing" closer to poetry than to the science of truth. If these considerations are legitimate, how do you look at the work of deconstruction, where the notion of "text" is extended to an interdisciplinary category applicable from metaphysics to the social sciences?

Nobody can verbalize the degree to which art perceives truth. At the level of pure intuition, I think that philosophy deals with materials—concepts, mental structures—of a less subjective nature than art. Philosophy moves on a more "fundamental" plane than art. Going back to Borges, I met him in Argentina, and, needless to say, I was quite excited about talking to him about all the philosophical themes he raises in his stories. Yet, all he wanted to do was to talk about Robert Louis Stevenson, and once he heard that I was a professor of philosophy, the last thing in the world he wanted to do was talk about anything philosophical.

What brought you to philosophy? Literature, science, or something else?

Some people say that adolescents spend a lot of time thinking about philosophical questions, and I can remember that at the age of thirteen or fourteen I thought about whether God exists, or if space ended. Then, sometime later, I wondered how we could justify our most basic moral principles. Sometime in high school I came across a paperback copy of Plato's *Republic,* which I didn't understand very well, but something about big ideas and big themes gripped me and made me think that I had found what I wanted to think about. I read some very good books early on in my life that brought me to philosophy. When I went to university I felt disoriented until I took one or two courses about contemporary social thought, which were taught by a philosophy professor. It was he who made me enthusiastic about philosophy. Every time I opened my mouth to say something, he would tell me that I had to make sharper distinctions and made objections to what I was saying. I valued such clear thinking and became drawn into the process of learning analytic philosophy.

Just a minute ago you admitted that you had a strong interest in the problematics pertinent to "scientific explanation," suggesting that your next book on rationality might again take up this concept.

When I named *Philosophical Explanations*, I was aware of paying a kind of homage to my teacher, Carl Hempel, who was the first to talk to me about scientific explanations.

Hempel is undoubtedly one of the old greats of analytic philosophy. Isn't it curious that you should take from him the key term of your noncoercive, and therefore in some way anti-analytic, discourse?

We never divorce ourselves completely from our backgrounds. I was willing to have multiple explanations rather than just one, so I was pluralistic about explanations, though I did want each explanation to meet certain rigorous standards. I mean, for me an explanation wasn't going to be just any illuminating remark, it was going to have a certain structure. There is something about intellectual structures that intrigues me. There are parts of mathematics that I use as analogies in philosophical work. That was very clear in *Anarchy, State, and Utopia* and in *Philosophical Explanations*. In fact, one of the things that worried me about *The Examined Life* was that I hadn't worked to create structures.

Then, you are not willing to recognize any friction between your pragmatically noncoercive universe and that of analytic philosophy?

That's a little too radical. I see the tension you refer to in the relationship between the emancipatory value of explanation and the coercive value it assumes in analytic discourse. However, if you compare explanation and argument, it is evident that the coercive potential of the former is much smaller than the latter. Moreover, explanations can be used very easily in a pluralistic concept. In explanation you have a considerable loosening of the argument that is the coercive potential of philosophy.

Then you propose a difference of degree, but not one of kind, between the noncoercive concept of explanation and the coercive notion of argumentation. Isn't this a rather literary way of defining the borders?

Let me once again go back to the relationship between philosophy and literature. When I was a sophomore or a junior, I chose philosophy over literature. I wasn't coming to philosophy through literature, but to philosophy as an alternative to literature. I was searching for a kind of intellectual satisfaction different from the narrative one.

Does the postmodern debate and the erosion of the border between literature and philosophy affect your choice?

I have followed the postmodern debate only from afar. While other people were discussing textuality, I was interested in the classical Indian philosophers. I was looking at a very different intellectual tradition and culture, something that would alter the way I thought

5

The Cosmopolitan
Alphabet of Art

Arthur C. Danto

A philosopher with strictly analytical training, a militant art critic, a professor, and a columnist, Arthur C. Danto reflects the quintessential polyvalence and disenchanted cosmopolitanism, of the New York intellectual scene.

Like the many artists who have guided his long itinerary as a scholar of aesthetics, Danto arrived in New York just after the Second World War, leaving for good Ann Arbor, a city not far from Detroit where he was born in 1924. His early work as a painter did not survive the war, which he spent as an American soldier in southern Italy. The encounter with philosophy took him almost by surprise, at Columbia University, where he has taught continuously for more than thirty years, apart from a brief stay in Colorado.

His whole reflection, spreading out in a sort of philosophical encyclopedism that extends from the moral terrain to the philosophy of history, from epistemology to the philosophy of art, has as its propelling center an "aestheticization" of the notion of conceptual structure, oriented in a neo-foundationalist perspective. His interest in the points of theoretical intersection between art and philosophy reflects this position, which takes its cue from a creative elaboration of analytic philosophy.

The rendezvous with analytic philosophy, inevitable for any American philosopher of his generation, came for Danto in the Rocky Mountains, on the occasion of his first university appointment, at the University of Colorado. From then onward he would never radically depart from this line of thought, even though he would not actually follow the trend of its American canonization.

Danto maintains a "foundationalist" reading of the analytic conceptual horizon, which consists in attributing to philosophy the role of reducing entities to their constitutive parts, almost along the lines of the anatomical perfection of an organism. This fascination with the "architectonic element" of thought represents the emergence of a fundamental need for "harmony." The instruments of logical analysis are the only ones capable of revealing the "beauty" which characterizes every coherent theoretical structure.

To disturb, disarrange, and recompose: these are the most frequent philosophical gestures in the mental horizon of Arthur C. Danto who, in this sense, is in profound disagreement with at least two lines of development in the "canonized" analytical thought. These are, first, the "therapeutical programs," (as he himself puts it) which use the instruments of analysis to free themselves from philosophy, convinced that, on the theoretical plane, one cannot but misunderstand language; and, second, the "idealistic programs" that are engaged in the compilation of an ideal language capable of embracing, as best it can, the formulation of scientific theories.

With the systematic rigor of a new thinker who has nourished himself on many traditions and has been enraptured, along the way, by more than one intellectual passion, Danto has taken the same "foundationalist" look at a multiplicity of disciplinary and cultural fields. The Analytical Philosophy of History (1965) represents his most emblematic contribution in the sphere of the philosophy of history, as the subsequent The Analytical Philosophy of Knowledge does for epistemology. Mysticism and Morality: Oriental Thought and Moral Philosophy (1972), bears witness to his attraction to the essentialism of oriental thought, which played a key role in the cultural debate of the sixties. The Transfiguration of the Commonplace (1981) and The Philosophical Disenfranchisement of the Art (1986) reveal a nucleus of reflection that appears more constant: that of the philosophical "recomprehension" of art.

While Danto accomplished the operation of aestheticizing the notion of conceptual structure in philosophy, in art he proceeded in a parallel way, trying to identify the philosophical nerve structure of the creative act. Starting from the Hegelian idea that a work of art embodies a "sensible materialization" of an idea, the philosophical dissection of the artistic object corresponds homologously to the dissection of conceptual structures, in both the procedures and the instrumentation.

Once again: to disarrange, disturb, and recompose are the dominant traits of Danto's aesthetic, which, not by chance, finds its archetype in that great disarrangement of artistic and philosophical sense consummated by the postwar American avant garde in pop art and New dada.

Art has never before scaled the peaks of philosophical creativity it reached in this "transfiguration of common sense," the definition that Danto applies to the conceptual structure, or philosophical foundation, embracing the radical experiences of such artists as Andy Warhol, Robert Motherwell, Roy Lichtenstein, and Robert Rauschenberg. Painting a series of soup cans (Warhol's *Campbell Soup Cans*) or disjointed comics (in the style of Lichtenstein) are mental operations that deviate so much from tradition and history that they become philosophical interrogations by which philosophy must let itself be guided by the hand.

*

From analytic philosophy to the philosophy of history to aesthetics: this is a complex itinerary, unforeseeable for a postwar American thinker. How do you explain it?

It's not such a wide range, to tell you the truth. The interest in history and the interest in art both go back a long way. I'll tell you the story. I planned to be a painter early in life. My passion for philosophy exploded much, much later, here in New York, where I moved in the middle of my undergraduate course of studies.

How do you remember the New York philosophical atmosphere of those years?

When I got to Columbia, it was a very old-fashioned place. I didn't know any better. I studied what I was taught and I got my first job at the University of Colorado. I was hired at the same time as two other young professors, one of them a student of Norman Malcolm and the other a student of Gilbert Ryle. It was the first time I learned anything about analytic philosophy, and I began to get really excited about that, and when I came back to Columbia, I came back with the idea that analytic philosophy was the most interesting thing that was happening. I was beginning to turn into a philosopher at that point.

And what happened to the painting?

There was a period of coexistence until the early sixties, which then all of a sudden stopped. It was interesting that in all that time, the early part of my career, I never wrote about aesthetics. I only wrote about aesthetics when, in the middle of the 1960s, art began to be, as I perceived it, philosophically interesting, and, as I have often written, it was through the kinds of things that Warhol and other conceptual pop artists were doing. My first paper was in 1964, and since then I've been writing rather steadily about aesthetics. By 1980, when *The Transfiguration of the Commonplace* was published, I began to have a fairly good theory of what I wanted. In that book I tried to pinpoint a series of philosophical questions the artistic avant garde was asking, questions which were undoubtedly new and disquieting for philosophy, and which the art world was happy to be told about. It was then that I was offered an art column in *The Nation,* and I became an art critic.

Your itinerary seems more like that of a European intellectual, accustomed to operating in many more fields, and speaking many more languages, than that of an American scholar raised in the pampered environment of the campus and a supporter of a strictly university-based intellectuality.

I am an analytic philosopher. I think that it is the right way to do philosophy, and I still practice it. It gave me a powerful sense of what the structure of a body of thought is, where things are joined almost as pieces of an anatomy, and I think it is a very, very beautiful way of thinking. I don't believe any longer in some of the positive and negative programs that motivated people to do analytical philosophy, neither the therapeutic programs—that is to say, we're going to get rid of philosophy by showing it is a misuse of language; nor the positive programs—that is, the construction of ideal languages which were supposed to house science. Both of them were visionary, but ultimately uninteresting. But analytic philosophy itself is the language I speak, in which I write and think. I prize clarity and exactness in writing.

If you had to draw a map of analytic philosophy, who would you consider the most prominent figure?

I have no heroes. . . . I'm not a disciple of any one particularly. I admire Donald Davidson. I admire Quine as a writer, and his early criticism of the analytic/synthetic distinction is, I think, one of the great moments in the history of twentieth-century philosophy; but there is a lot of Quine that I think is sort of poor. I admire Nelson Goodman as a moralist of philosophical thought, but his programs seem to me to be laughably inadequate. At one point, I got a great deal out of Russell and the early Wittgenstein. The later Wittgenstein strikes me as hazy: it is beautifully written, marvelous thought, but philosophically of no significance whatsoever.

What was your background before your encounter with analytic philosophy?

I couldn't avoid Dewey's influence, he was a big deal at that time. He's getting to be a big deal again. But, from the very beginning I thought he was just awful, just muddy, like a preacher, portentous and uninteresting. I still think a lot of that is true, but I think analytic philosophy enables one to see Dewey as one of the main systems, a somewhat "holistic" system. In Dewey as a writer, I don't have much interest, and in this I am in complete disagreement with Rorty. I don't see any structure in him, while I have passion for the architecture of philosophical thought.

What do you mean by "architecture of philosophical thought?"

I like things to be clear, I like connections to be clear, and I like to see structures, whereas with Dewey it's an unstructured world in which you sort of move through a fog. However, I feel that you can, from a certain distance, begin to see where Dewey replaces structure with fog. And you can understand why he does it, what the systematic reasons are, and if you take a sufficiently distant view of that, you can see that the lack of structure is one of the great historic alternatives to clarity. But it is not the way that I would want to do philosophy. I'm something of an eighteenth-century person, I really do see this as an ordered universe. . .

Would you extend your accusation of obscurity to other currents of thought in those years? For example, the Frankfurt school, which, starting with 1935, moved to New York and precisely to Columbia University?

The Frankfurt school never had a real academic position here. They were a research institute at Columbia, where they had a little cell on 114th Street. They never entered the mainstream of American philosophy, and they had a very European way of thinking about things. At the time, it seemed that people hadn't yet figured out what the philosophical importance of logic was, whereas the logical positivists came in with logic, in which there was spontaneously going to be a lot of interest. The members of the Frankfurt school didn't have real academic jobs; they didn't really penetrate intellectual life in the United States at all.

What about *One-Dimensional Man,* by Herbert Marcuse, and *The Sexual Revolution,* by Wilhelm Reich, both of which, in the sixties, became cult books for an entire generation?

Both have been very important, but not for philosophers: Marcuse for political theory, Reich for psychoanalysis. Analytic philosophy also had a scientific aura that the Frankfurt school never succeeded in achieving. To the outside world it looked as though people who were doing analytical work were doing something scientific. I think that, in the United States, unless it looks as though you are doing something scientific, and therefore useful, it's very difficult to get grants and academic employment. Therefore, step by step, the universities just got to be filled by people who did analytic philosophy. Students were trained that way, and, after a while, that got to be what philosophy *was* in the United States, for a very long time. And the difficulty with that is, I think, that philosophy didn't undergo a real evolution. The truth of the matter is that people doing analytic philosophy today are not doing anything remarkably different from what they did twenty or thirty years ago. A tiny bit, but not much.

Then what do you foresee as new points of departure? Do you think that the return to a greater philosophical "narrative," of

the type suggested by the neo-pragmatism of Richard Rorty, could be a guiding path?

It is difficult to predict, especially because of our academic inertia. If you are doing philosophy in the United States today, you've got to go through graduate school. And if you're going to go through graduate school and get a job, you're going to have to be approved by people in the profession. I imagine that philosophical education for a very long time is going to be logical and analytic, and therefore philosophical writing is going to be like that for a very long time.

On the basis of these considerations one could account for the absolute lack of success of a part of European philosophy in the philosophy departments and, on the contrary, its success in the literature departments. I refer, for example, to the deconstruction of Jacques Derrida, the post-structuralism of Lyotard and Gilles Deleuze, and the hermeneutics of Hans Georg Gadamer.

This does not only concern European philosophy, but also those few Americans who, like Richard Rorty, dared to renege on their analytic past. Since he published *Philosophy and the Mirror of Nature,* Rorty has embraced neo-pragmatism, becoming very famous too, and he no longer belongs to a department of philosophy. He belongs instead to a literary interdisciplinary program. When he was at Princeton he really began to dislike the analytical tone of the philosophy department and was anxious to leave it. But other people don't feel that way. I love the company of philosophers.

I deduce that you are not at all anxious that American philosophy "free" itself from the logical and analytic game.

I'm anxious to see philosophy liberalized in certain ways, but I'm not interested in seeing the curriculum changed very much. I think it's essential to do interesting original work, to know how to handle a philosophical argument and to present a thesis with clarity and logical support.

The problem is to establish whether clarity derives from pure logical architecture rather than from historical explanation. One of the problems of analytic philosophy is that it completely marginalizes the history of ideas.

Columbia, at least, has always had an interest in the history of philosophy. I think most departments are interested in some sense in the history of philosophy. Not archivally, you might say, but people are supposed to at least understand what Kant was trying to do, what Descartes, Plato, or Aristotle were trying to do.

What effects do you think these differences between the European and American "formations" have on the production of original philosophical views?

Once you have passed your first paper, your second paper, your first book, you begin to write for yourself, you try to write freely. I don't think that there is going to be an awful lot of difference at that point, for we all find ourselves alone, alone with philosophy.

The disparity between traditions, however, remains a problem of intellectual communication. Europeans think that Americans are closed in a desperate dream of scientific objectivity. Americans see Europeans as visionary metaphysicians. American philosophy is received in Europe in narrow spaces of debate, limited to professors of logic and philosophy of language. In America, European philosophy is watered down by an essentially literary use. Don't you think the moment has come to abandon the wall of the Atlantic?

I like to think that authors can communicate. Take Donald Davidson, who is always invited to speak all over the world. People want to know what he is thinking. They never say, "Oh Davidson, he's only interested in language." Well, people find the questions Donald is interested in extremely inspiring, classical questions like the weakness of will, the issue of metaphor, the structure of rationality. How much history they know does not matter.

One of the problems of analytic philosophy remains the use of a very technical language that cuts off anyone who is not really a part of it, including philosophers of a different background.

Sure it could happen, it all depends on how you do it. In the case of analytic philosophy, it is very much related to a question of style. Analytic papers follow the style of a scientific report. There is a rhetoric attached to that, there's no question about it. But there's a rhetoric attached to almost every kind of philosophical writing, and

I think it's a good idea to try and become conscious of this rhetoric. Europeans cannot renounce the big, fat three-volume *Gesamtwerk*. That's a piece of rhetoric too. There are issues of style operative at every point, and if one finds out what the style of rhetoric is, what the style of philosophical expression is, one will probably also find out answers to all the institutional questions that there are. Then you've got to decide if you are interested in impressing your colleagues, or in reaching another kind of audience altogether. I think those are very difficult questions we face as human beings, not just as academics. It's a matter of confidence and a certain amount of cynicism.

These considerations are particularly significant in light of your journalistic experience, an isolated case among American scholars. How do you reconcile the two experiences?

From the beginning, it was just as easy as could be, and it was interesting. I deeply loved writing in itself. Diderot was a philosopher who wrote art criticism, and he found it enormously liberating. I mean, he did it for ten years. . . I don't know of any other philosopher who has tried to be a practicing art critic. Maybe Benedetto Croce.

The extra-philosophical passion of Croce may have been more literary than figurative.

Yes, it's true. There are not many philosophers who were art critics also. That makes it even more interesting. To write about art, for a philosopher, is such a liberating experience. . .

Have you ever considered literature? After all, as an aesthetician, art would seem a more compact field than you recognize. What does the priority of figurative art represent for you? And why not literature?

I write about literature now and then, when chances come up. I just don't think that literature has been as powerfully interesting from a philosophical point of view as painting has been, because painting has been through all these incredible conceptual revolutions since the late 1880s—for the past century, you might say.

Whereas, I think any reader of Dickens would not have that much difficulty reading novels today, I'm sure that somebody who grew up in the nineteenth century would have very great difficulty understanding what's going on in Soho. Painting is quite a different world.

Judging from your writing, the revolution of the avant garde after the Second World War is the one you have followed most closely, and especially the line of "conceptual" experimentation inaugurated by Andy Warhol and pop art. But why not other currents, such as minimalism or abstract expressionism?

Warhol was for me the most interesting figure. I had a very powerful experience when I worked at an exhibition in 1964, when he showed those *Brillo Boxes* for the first time. I discovered Claes Oldenburg, Robert Rauschenberg, Roy Lichtenstein. I found them stimulating in a way, in a philosophical way, in which I had never found anything before, not even in Willem De Kooning or Jackson Pollock. I never would have written philosophically about art if hadn't been for them, and they raised all these deep questions for me, like, why did this happen at this time? How was it historically possible that people would begin to paint soup cans and Brillo boxes and make tee shirts and comic strip panels, and it would be considered fine art? That seemed to me like a marvelous question to be answered.

If you could reconfigure your dreams as an adolescent and as a young aspiring painter, would you choose to become Andy Warhol?

Among my fantasies were Cézanne, Filippo Lippi, and Masaccio. It's just that I had never thought of them philosophically. I think this has been a great period to think philosophically about art, because art has been so philosophically creative. Since 1964, art has become so different from anything it was before that almost everything written philosophically about art before that time is worthless. Many philosophers who thought they were doing philosophy were in fact doing some sort of art criticism.

Until now, you seem to attribute philosophical creativity only to a part of the postwar avant garde, and in particular to the New York axis of pop art. What would you say of the Franco-

American line of the New dada? Don't you think that, from a
philosophical point of view, the "transfiguration of the commonplace" is expressed even more radically by neo-dadaist works
such as Duchamp's "ready-made," and Rauschenberg's and Lou-
ise Nevelson's "found-objects". . .

I give a lot of credit to Duchamp, although I don't think that he is
somebody who could have been understood until 1960. But I agree
with you. Both pop art and New dada raise the same questions on
the nature of art and the nature of history, questions that have
accompanied my philosophical itinerary throughout.

Andy Warhol always considered the management of his personal image, his public presence, his life style, as an "artistic
event," the equivalent of the production of a work of art. Warhol treated himself as an art object, completely reified and
"ready-made," mass-produced merchandise, lacking subjective intensity—an interesting operation from the aesthetic point of
view but, I imagine, very difficult to sustain in personal relationships. Where did you meet Warhol?

Where else if not at a party? We were really two different species.
I couldn't talk to him, he couldn't talk to me. I found he had an
extraordinary philosophical intelligence. He was consistently brilliant about everything, and everything he made was philosophically
amazing, but I don't think he could talk about it philosophically.
So my personal experience of him was from a distance, across a
room, at a party.

I believe that the philosophical interest of pop art and New
dada lies in the problematization of the conceptual boundaries
of art. The boundaries between art and life are blurred, thanks
to the practice of displacement, the dislocation of the use-value
of an ordinary object (such as Warhol's can of Campbell's soup
and Duchamp's urinal) elevated to an object of artistic consump-
tion. This erosion of the demarcation line between art and life
has allowed for some speculation about the "death" or the "disappearance" of art. Many critics and philosophers of different
schools have in fact taken up this theme and have elaborated it
in different forms. I'm thinking especially of Harold Rosenberg

and, on the European scene, Jean Baudrillard. What is your position on this issue?

Personally, I never believed in the disappearance of art, and I don't have any idea as to how it could happen philosophically. I think that nobody has ever talked better about art than Hegel, and when he talks about artistic beauty as the idea given sensuous embodiment, I think that's about as good as you can get. As long as sensuous embodiment is essential, I don't think that art can ever become, as it were, pure abstraction. Not even abstract art escapes the materialization of the sensible. Philosophically speaking, the disappearance of art is not possible; but this does not mean that, from an experimental point of view, it is uninteresting to see how far you can go in that direction.

Earlier, regarding your attraction for analytic philosophy, you spoke of a love for conceptual structures, for their transparency and their anatomy. If one were trying to give a comprehensive definition of your thought, would it be wrong to speak of a type of structuralism?

I'm talking about foundationalism in some way: something fairly reduced to its constituent parts. Foundationalism seems correct, and I think it's the way the mind is built. I like the idea of being able to break things down and put them back together. I like to observe how the different elements interconnect and function. I'm not so sure that all paintings work along those lines. But I'm talking about this as a writer, as a thinker. I like to break problems down and then solve them. And I am well aware that this is a very Cartesian image.

Foundationalism, then, is also the key to reading the aesthetic significance of the postwar avant garde, including pop art?

Yes, that's right.

I imagine you realize that your position is neither very strong nor very widely shared. The philosophical and aesthetic inheritance of the avant garde in the last twenty years has in fact oriented itself toward an anti-foundationalist elaboration, deconstructive and hermeneutic, from the galaxy of post-structuralism in France, to American postmodernism, to Italian weak thought.

Even in the art world, the effects of the pop and neo-dada conceptual revolution have been everything but "foundationalist." If one thinks of performance art, mixed-media, body art, and all the other forms of conceptualism, there is no doubt that together they express a nihilistic vision, centered on the crisis of some "fundamental" notion such as that of a constitutive structure or subject.

Performance art has gotten into certain notions of "ephemeralization." There are institutional criticisms of art, people taking stands about the museum, the gallery, the art world, things that are supposed to be of beauty and joy forever. And although I think that those are very important criticisms, I do think that, at the level of a philosophical analysis of art, the "ephemeralization" is itself pretty ephemeral.

Many American postwar artists have taken a profound interest in the culture of the "other," especially Eastern culture. In particular, the "otherness" has been recognized as an alternative to the society of technological mass-production and consumer alienation. It is precisely in those years that you wrote *Mysticism and Morality*. How do you reconcile your foundationalist perspective with your interest in Eastern philosophy?

The East had already been in the air since the fifties. Dr. Suzuki, who after all was a great Zen master, used to teach right down the hall, here at Columbia University. I thought that Suzuki's seminars were a little like Kojeve's seminars on the "existentialist" Hegel in Paris. Everybody came to hear Dr. Suzuki, and I think Zen ideas penetrated very deeply into New York consciousness at that time. I got very involved in thinking about the East. In my book on mysticism, I remember telling about my visit to the first wonderful show of Japanese art in the immediate postwar years. Going from one room to another, I came across a series of Venetian paintings, which I was surprised to find disgustingly fat. I could not stand that water, air, light.

Do you still read any Eastern literature?

Still today I often think of a wonderful Taoist image, described by Chuan-Tze. The scene takes place at a butcher's shop where there's a carcass hanging. The king is watching the butcher, and the butcher with just one move makes the carcass fall in pieces. The king says, "How do you do that? You don't seem to put any effort into it." And the butcher says, "I studied Tao, and when you study Tao you know how things fit together."

Is this your idea of philosophy: to disarrange and rearrange the order of the world?

This is an image of profound philosophical inspiration. But the story is not over, for the butcher adds, "Between two bones, there's an empty space, and the knife goes into emptiness. When you put emptiness within emptiness, the knife never goes dull, and everything falls apart." That's what philosophy should be. You should be able to break problems up in that nice way. If you know where the joints are, it should fall almost effortlessly apart. I found those metaphors very beautiful, but I stopped believing in Eastern thought. I was very interested in it for a long time and there are still things that move me, like the *Bhaguvadgita* and the *I-Ching* However, I don't think they are more wonderful than any other thing I believe in.

I have always suspected that the interest of American artists and intellectuals in the East has been in some way predetermined by a peculiar form of naturalism, in which the United States has been saturated since its dawn. It suffices to think about Emerson, who demonstrated a profound enthusiasm for Buddhist philosophy; and then, in the twentieth century, of the organicist poetics of the architecture of Frank Lloyd Wright, an untiring admirer of the Japanese sense of space.

I see what you mean. I'm sure that's true. Frank Lloyd Wright was certainly gripped by Japanese paradigms. But the Orient is a pretty big place: it's difficult to see Indian temples as having much of an influence on America. And "Japanism" had a kind of aesthetic impact not just here, but all over, from the 1880s onward.

Moving on from the Orient to old Europe. . .

I have always loved Europe. I was a soldier in Italy from the invasion of Salerno until the end of the war, so that's a long time. I met lots of people, but I met the kinds of people that soldiers meet. I learned a very coarse Italian, and although those were very difficult times, I thought the people were magnificent. It was a very powerful experience, humanly speaking.

In contrast with many Americans who encountered Europe through the great capitals, you experienced it in its more residual version, poor, and certainly not cosmopolitan.

That's true. But when I returned to Europe in 1949 I went to Paris, and that was marvelous too because all the great artists were still alive, life was very cheap, and I suppose that every American who went there thought it was a place where a form of life was available that wasn't possible in the United States.

Yet, in those years, New York was also a stimulating place.

It was indeed. I went back to New York in 1950 and didn't return to Europe for ten years. Then I became immersed in European cultural life, whereas today I am more detached from places—I don't think it matters whether you go to Nairobi or Budapest or Milan. It probably takes a long time to penetrate any of those cities, but on the level at which one lives they are all pretty much the same.

Has your relationship with European intellectuals also weakened?

In the seventies, in France, I knew many people, including Jacques Derrida and Jacques Lacan. But I don't have real friends. The language of French intellectuals has always seemed to me barbarous and intolerable.

You refer to the group of structuralists who slid into post-structuralism: aside from Derrida and Lacan, also Claude Lévi-Strauss and Michel Foucault.

I remember as a characteristic of those years the fact that all important intellectual events were accompanied by an awful amount of frivolity, whereas I'm convinced that one really needs a certain amount of analytic discipline to carry out the next step. I don't think they knew how to elaborate on those ideas, even if their thoughts were profound. The idea of how things hang together, the notions of paradigm and of text, the idea of the mind as a text, of history as a text: all these are very deep ideas, but I don't think anybody has done anything with them yet.

I imagine that you would express the same judgment on all Derridean-style deconstructionists: Philippe Lacoue-Labarthe, Jean-Luc Nancy, and the many Americans who sided with them, including Yale thinkers such as Paul de Man, Geoffrey Hartman, and Jay Hillis Miller. Your essays on deconstruction are incandescent.

Deconstruction has just become a slogan for people. It's difficult to see what it means. I'm pretty sure most of it has to be false, that is to say, the idea of interpretation being endless, there being no such thing as truth. I think interpretation is fine, and there had better be something like truth.

And how do you evaluate the metaphysics of deconstruction as advanced by Derrida in Writing and Difference and in Of Grammatology?

I think he was wrong and perverse from the start. I think the whole question about the metaphysics of presence never has any clear answer. Sometimes Derrida just pins a label on the texts: he deconstructs them, but he is never interested in examining the metaphysics of presence in a philosophical sense. It is not enough to take texts apart and deconstruct them. Derrida never confronts questions like the metaphysics of presence by really dealing with those questions philosophically. He never takes anything apart or puts it together; he just takes a text, the more obscure the better, deconstructs it, and goes on to the next text. I ask myself, what am I doing this for? What am I getting out of it? What is mankind getting out of it? Derrida does not believe in taking second steps, and I think it's a bad example—I mean a bad example for others less strong than he is.

How do you explain the success of deconstruction in America? Is it because of the opposition of the philosophers that, on this side of the Atlantic, deconstruction has become a methodology of literary criticism? a way of reading texts, and of writing about texts, based on the maxim, "nothing outside the text."

If there is nothing outside the text, we're taking some stand outside the text anyway. So from now on it's a question of what's inside, what's outside. And I don't think we can live with that.

6

After Philosophy, Democracy

Richard Rorty

In the panorama of contemporary American philosophy, Richard Rorty represents an exception. Perhaps not since his ideal teacher, John Dewey, has the United States produced such an intellectual phenomenon: a well-rounded thinker in the European style, versatile, optimistic, and engaged in public debate, rather than an American-style professional philosopher.

Philosophy and the Mirror of Nature (1979) gained Rorty international renown as the founder of "neo-pragmatism." Since then, he has ceaselessly amazed the philosophical community by betraying the model of its "professional" training. In 1983, after teaching for fifteen years in the philosophical citadel of Princeton, Rorty decided to move to an interdisciplinary department of the University of Virginia, seemingly picking up again the radical thread of his origins in New York, where he was born in 1931 to two old-guard socialist writers. Furthermore, he assumes an extremely discursive style of thought and writing, a grand conceptual gesture that, faithful to the American and democratic tradition of pragmatism and liberalism, cannot but oppose itself to the rigor of the analytic genre, which is more inclined to the work of minute argumentation than to the construction of vast speculative syntheses.

The point of departure of Rorty's neo-pragmatist discourse is precisely a critique of analytic philosophy. However, he directs his criticism mainly at its first phase, the most orthodox one, born following the immigration of Viennese logical positivism to the United States. In fact, a second phase of analyticism, embracing authors such as Quine and Davidson, whose proximity to pragmatism is emphasized by Rorty, remains untouched by his attack. To their post-analytic reading Rorty attributes the merit of having brought the notion of logical analysis, central to the whole analytic discourse, "to commit a slow suicide"—an operation that neopragmatism would have brought to completion in a historical key instead.

According to Rorty, the sin committed by the first phase of analytic thought, which remains dominant in the American field even today, resides in the "professionalization" of philosophy, that restricts its purview to that of an academic discipline, with a shared neo-Kantian orientation reflected in a legalistic style limited exclusively to epistemological discourse.

In Rorty's view, the analytic philosophers thus embarked on a genuine anti-historicist obsession, with two results. On the one hand, the denial of any historical perspective to their work; and, on the other, the demonization of that line of thought stretching from Hegel's idealist turn through several developments in Continental philosophy—including Freud, Nietzsche, and Heidegger—that have been interpreted as dark and metaphysical ways of thought, not to mention a nihilistic threat to scientific reason.

Yet, it is precisely in this line, to which Wittgenstein and the American pragmatists belong, that Rorty finds the only prospect for resurrecting the philosophical project or, at least, for inserting it into what, in *Consequences of Pragmatism,* he defines as "post-analytical culture."

A distinctive trait of the new post-philosophical picture is the translation of the category of objectivity into that of solidarity. Philosophy, involved in a process of "humanistic" de-disciplinization, no longer retains the role of mother and queen of the sciences, ever in search of a definitive and immortal vocabulary on the basis of which to synthesize or discard the results of other spheres of activity. Rather, it becomes democratized in the form of a "cultural criticism" that sees itself transformed into one discipline among others, founded on historically and socially contextual criteria and emphasizing the comparative study of the advantages and disadvantages of the various perspectives on the world. Pluralism and secularization therefore represent the keys with which this new reality closes and locks up the shop of modern metaphysics, of epistemology and foundationalism.

A pragmatism drawing on various disciplinary idioms, together with a hermeneutics completely de-ontologized of history, redesigns the operative space of the philosophical profession: philosophy does not aim at being a science but at pursuing a Socratic, *maieutic* project of edification. "Maieutic" in its sense of commitment to the relativity of every theoretical effort, that is, to making us doubt the "modern" values of system and foundation and convincing us instead of the postmodern values of proliferation and plurality.

In his last book, *Philosophy after Philosophy: Contingency, Irony, Solidarity*, Rorty intersects the categories of contingency and solidarity with that of irony, which he paints as a strictly philosophical domain. Irony represents the disenchanted pose that the new type of thinker, the "ironic liberal," must assume in order to become "sufficiently historicist and nominalist" to realize the contingency of his most profound convictions. As Socratic as he is Voltairean, the philosopher of neo-pragmatism is at the service of "liberal utopia," which he believes is not so much the destiny of human nature or of history, as simply the best idea that men have produced from the objectives for which they work. Solidarity thus is not discovered through the systematic rigor of reflection; rather, it is created, allowed to flow out, from the transgressive value of irony.

*

Europe always searches for well-rounded philosophers who are versatile and engaged in public debate. Accordingly, you have been assigned the role of "teacher of neo-pragmatism," a sort of reincarnation of John Dewey.

Dewey was the dominant intellectual figure in America in my youth. He was often called the philosopher of democracy, of the New Deal, of the American democratic intellectuals. If one attended an American university any time before 1950, it would have been impossible not to be aware of him. I think that he was a remarkable man. He started out as an Evangelical Christian, then he became a Hegelian, then he read Darwin and he sort of dropped Christianity to try to put together Darwin and Hegel. His philosophy is a kind of naturalization of Hegel—Hegel without the split between nature and spirit. Just as Hegel's philosophy was a kind of secularized Christianity, so Dewey's was a sort of Christian social hope combined with a Darwinian way of looking at human beings.

But what can Dewey contribute to a philosopher like you, approaching the end of the millennium?

What I find attractive about Dewey, now that I'm older, is his criticism of Platonism, of Cartesianism, of Kant, of the whole tradition of metaphysics that Derrida and Heiddeger oppose. His criticism, however, sprang from an optimistic social perspective, since he didn't think that the end of metaphysics was a matter of despair or nihilism. He thought that ending metaphysics could be done gradually, in the way we have gradually got rid of theology. Dewey thought that liberating culture from theological considerations and from metaphysical dualisms was a good idea. He was aware that it would take a long time to accomplish, and that it would be the final stage in the secularization of culture.

How would you define the difference in perspective between Deweyan pragmatism and your neo-pragmatism?

I don't think there is any great difference in fundamentals. I pay close attention to the philosophy of language, while Dewey did not. It is a matter of intellectual context, and I was brought up on analytic philosophy, particularly the philosophy of language. Within analytic philosophy, Dewey's themes—or, better yet, Dewey's attacks on traditional dualisms—have been persuasively presented in the form of doctrines in the philosophy of language, particularly by Quine and Davidson. I don't think this adds anything much to Dewey: it is just adapting what Dewey said for a different audience, for people with different expectations.

When was your first encounter with logical analysis?

I was briefly a student of Carnap and of Hempel, but they were not my principal teachers. My training had been predominantly historical. My encounter with analytic philosophy took place at

Princeton, when I was already teaching. It was an exciting period. Wittgenstein's later work was just being assimilated, and Quine and Sellars were writing their most important material.

What was Wittgenstein's role in the analytic realm in the United States?

I first read Wittgenstein in the late fifties, as a sort of relief from Reichenbach. Wittgenstein played the role of a pragmatist within the philosophy of language, decentralizing philosophy of language itself. Wittgenstein was a threatening figure because he contributed substantially to *de*transcendentalizing and *de*professionalizing philosophy. Hence, academic philosophers in America and England always had an ambiguous reaction to him. On the one hand, he is obviously the greatest figure in the field; on the other, he is a danger to the profession. All this aside, Wittgenstein has a great appeal for me. As Stanley Cavell says, what's remarkable about the two great philosophers of the twentieth century is that Wittgenstein writes as if he had read nothing, while Heidegger writes as if he had read everything.

Why did American philosophy open itself with such enthusiasm to European émigrés between the two wars?

Americans simply had not produced anything in philosophy for a long time. Dewey's best work had been written before 1925, hence for twenty-five years not much had happened in American philosophy—though Dewey was still alive and revered. In the thirties, the German and Austrian émigrés began coming over—people like Carnap, Hempel, Tarski, Reichenbach—and, after the Second World War, they simply took over American philosophy departments. They were an explicitly anti-historicist movement, attempting to make philosophy scientifically, rather than historically, oriented.

What was the reason for this opposition to historicism, so quickly assimilated by American philosophy?

The logical positivists thought that fascism was associated with anti-science, and that respect for science and scientific method was the mark of anti-fascism in philosophical thought. Heidegger's identification with the Nazis was important for Carnap because he saw

Heidegger's "historicity of Being" and his Nazism as somehow connected. When Carnap came to the United States he imported the
belief that philosophy had to be defended from historicism and
Nazism by avoiding thinkers like Plato, Hegel, and Nietzsche. Karl
Popper presented the same view in his book *The Open Society,* which
was an extremely influential book in America. Popper thought that
Plato, Hegel, and Marx were totalitarian thinkers, and that we had
to avoid their style of thought and embrace a more modern, up-to-
date and scientific way of thinking. This was a very powerful ideological rhetoric, still believed by most American philosophers, who
are convinced that political and moral decency is a matter of respect
for scientific rationality.

**Do you believe that the same fate lies in store for hermeneutics
in the United States? I refer mainly to the hermeneutic historicism of Gadamer, who is at the center of a great part of the European debate.**

I don't think so. Hermeneutics isn't a term we use much in America:
we prefer to talk about "Continental philosophy," which includes
everyone from Gadamer to Lyotard. However, I do not think that
the term hermeneutics has a uniform interpretation in Europe either. In the sixties and seventies it was widely discussed in France
and in Germany; today it has been replaced by post-structuralism.

**If you had to write a history of American philosophy, when
would you locate its beginning?**

I would certainly emphasize the sharp break of the fifties, the development of analytic philosophy, which is a different kind of philosophy. The question of where to locate its beginning is still open.
Many American philosophers—Royce and Santayana—have not left
a school of followers.

What about Emerson?

Emerson was never read by philosophers as a philosopher. Before
Heidegger, Nietzsche also wasn't considered a philosopher. Only
recently have people like Stanley Cavell and Cornell West tried to
bring Emerson into the philosophical canon. Emerson and Thoreau
were considered literary figures in the tradition of American eccen-
trics.

Dewey appears to be an exception in the American panorama: he left a school; he reconciled, so to speak, the logic of the monastery with that of the city, reawakening in American thought an interest in questions of an ethico-social order.

American culture is essentially political. America was founded upon an ethical concept of freedom. It was founded as the land of the freest society, the place where democracy is at its best, where the horizons are open. There is a kind of national romance about a country that says, "We are different from Europe because we made a fresh start. We don't have traditions, we can create human beings as they are supposed to be." I think that the romanticism about America runs through from Emerson to Dewey. Unfortunately, it has been lost. It's been lost quite recently, around the time of the Vietnam War.

You identify the intellectual identity of the United States as an interrupted "national romance." But what is happening today?

Old socialists, like Sidney Hook, are among the few American intellectuals involved in this sort of social romanticism. I think that the romance of American life had a lot to do with our sense that we were the country of the future. Then it gradually turned out that this was the end of American dominance and that we were no longer the biggest, richest country. Suddenly, it was as if the intellectuals turned sour and as if they had been deceived.

Why should it have been interrupted with the Vietnam War?

There had been two previous wars fought by Americans: the Mexican-American War and the Spanish-American War. These wars were denounced by intellectuals because it looked as if we were becoming merely European, that is, just one more imperialist power. The intellectuals looked favorably upon the First and Second World Wars because they were fought to defeat the forces of evil. Hence, after the Second World War, the American intellectuals could feel very proud of their country's historical role: things like the Marshall Plan gave a sense of a better world to come. The Vietnam War changed all that. This was a completely unjust war. It wasn't even imperialism. We were simply trying to take over a country for the sake of its natural resources—we were killing people in a mindless way. Somehow we never recovered from it. Also, it was the first time we had ever been defeated in war. We were sort of defeated in the Korean War, but not intellectually. For the first time in two hundred years we had lost a war, and the people started to think that we were not God's country after all.

Do you believe that religion has played an important role in the national self-determination of the United States?

At times, but not dominantly. Thoreau and Whitman weren't religious. Surely, religion became important at the beginning of the twentieth century, the time of the so-called social gospel, a sort of social-democratic Christianity. The Protestant churches in the north took the lead in social reforms. It resurfaced in the sixties with the Civil Rights movement and Martin Luther King.

Let's now try to switch places, and to look at Europe from the United States. Who is the "Continental" author who has had the most influence on your philosophy?

I would say, Martin Heidegger. I first read him in the late fifties because I was curious about what was happening in Europe.

Which Heidegger interested you most: the existential Heidegger of *Being and Time,* or the hermeneutic Heidegger of *Holzwege*?

At the beginning, the only work we knew about was *Being and Time.* Until the early sixties, even in Europe, Heidegger meant *Being and Time.*

In Italy today, some philosophers, like Gianni Vattimo, tend to unite the two phases of Heideggerian thought into a single curve, thereby incorporating the existential Heidegger into a new post-metaphysical perspective. What do you think?

I agree. I prefer to think that Heidegger struggled all his life to reach one objective: self-overcoming. The *Letter on Humanism* repudiates *Being and Time* in the same way that *What is thinking?* repudiates the *Letter on Humanism.* This is significant for the "Heidegger case" and his relationship to Nazism. The fact is that between European and American philosophy there is no continuity. American intellectuals forgot about philosophy until the sixties, when people like Habermas, Gadamer, Foucault, and Derrida reminded them. However, that does not mean that there was an actual interaction.

Why do you attribute this role to Derrida, Foucault, and Habermas, and not to Marcuse and Adorno? that is to say, to the preceding generation that, aside from immigrating to the United States, also regularly taught here?

They were and they weren't here. They were here in body, but not in spirit, since they never noticed America, and the things they used to say about America were just absurd. They lived here in exile without really believing that this was a real country. I think that to get caught up on Adorno and Marcuse one has to take Marx more seriously than he has ever been taken in America. Derrida, Foucault, and Heiddeger don't ask you to take Marx all that seriously. Before the sixties we had no Marxist tradition; in the United States people simply didn't read Marx, people still don't read Marx.

Among the authors of so-called French post-structuralism, Foucault seems to be the one you have identified with most.

He was a remarkable man; he had a great imagination, and he wrote memorable books. Foucault has been the most influential figure on the culture of the American left, but his influence has been dangerous. The result has been the "disengagement" of intellectuals: the idea was to resist the bio-power exercised by capitalist society, but without any political notion of how to resist, without any political program, without any political utopia. Foucault's effect on the American intellectual community has been one of profound resentment.

In Italy, Foucault's influence has been remarkable both in the intellectual debate and in the major institutional reforms that revolutionized psychiatry in the sixties, and, more generally, the structure of mental hospitals.

We also closed our mental hospitals, but not because of Foucault. He's read by the literary intelligentsia, not by the medical people. Doctors don't take him seriously.

Marx has been of fundamental importance for all the French post-structuralist authors: Lyotard, Deleuze, Virilio, and also Foucault. Have you ever read Marx?

My parents' home was full of Marx. They read him, so I read him as a kid, but not as a philosopher. I still can't read him as a philosopher.

Does this have any influence on your reading of Habermas and on his recent American assimilation into the postmodern perspective? I'm thinking of Fredric Jameson, in particular, and about his idea of a "political unconscious" in the consumer society.

When Habermas says that he is a Marxist, I can't imagine how or why, since he does not sound like one. He sounds like an ordinary Deweyan liberal. There is a kind of piety in European thought, by which you must not turn your back on Marx. You must find something good in Marx, somewhere, if only in the early manuscripts. This has never been the case in America. I mean, nobody cares whether you have read Marx—not even Fredric Jameson.

Marxism, then, is simply a distinctly European heritage?

There are two barriers dividing American and European thought. The first is that Americans have read fewer history books and know less about the history of ideas than Europeans. The other is the American reception of Marx.

The optimistic thrust of your philosophy clashes with the crepuscular, decadent, and somewhat nostalgic tone of our Continental *esprit du temps*. In fact, philosophical hermeneutics, trans-avant-gardism, and neo-romanticism in music, are all movements that attribute a new centrality to memory and citation, understood as a privileged channel of access to history.

If in hermeneutics you include "weak thought," which I am familiar with, we have to be clear about it. Neither Dewey nor weak thought imply that history is on our side, or that there is any necessary force that's going to cause a good outcome. On the contrary, there are nine chances out of ten that things will go to hell. However, what is important is the hope that they might not end badly, because they are not fated to go one way or the other. There is not just one Hegelian story of progress, or one Hedeggerian story of nihilism to be told.

One of your most debated definitions, that of post-philosophical culture, reproposes the problem of trans-disciplinarity, both at the theoretical and institutional level.

This problem is a reaction against the scientific notion of philosophy. Philosophy is not a quasi-scientific discipline: once you think of philosophy as continuous with literature you give up disciplinary segmentation. It seems to me that Europeans have been reading philosophy as continuous with literature for a long time. Valéry and Sartre could wander back and forth between the two as they wished. This is a desirable situation, not to have to worry about whether you are writing philosophy or literature. But, in American academic culture, that's not possible, because you have to worry about the department you are in.

In defining the post-philosophical perspective, it seems to me that you want to link the dissolution of the barrier between philosophy and literature to the notion of *narrative*. What do you mean by this?

I relate it mainly to the difference between Kant and Hegel, between the *Critique of Pure Reason* and the *Phenomenology of Spirit*. It seems to me that in the *Phenomenology*, and in Hegel's early writings, there is a kind of philosophical writing that is narrative in form; it is basically a story about the history of human nature. I believe that's become the dominant mode of philosophical thought, except in the academy. In the universities you can't write narratives, you have to pretend to be studying some subject—the nature of a text, the nature of signs, the nature of science. This strikes me as somewhat phony.

Yet in your last book, *Contingency, Irony, and Solidarity* you state that authors like Derrida, who is not an analytic thinker, write books that are limited to a reading public of philosophers because others would lack the necessary points of reference to understand them.

Not exactly philosophers, but people who haven't read the previous history of philosophy. If you have gone to a gymnasium, the Italian *liceo* or the French *lycée*, where philosophy is part of the ordinary curriculum for at least three years, you will be able to follow a philosophical argument. But I write for an English-speaking audience, and, typically, well-educated English and American people won't be able to follow what Derrida is talking about, because they can't catch the allusions.

The problem of writing stories on philosophy, of writing about philosophy as an author, then translates itself into the problem of the reader: whom do we write for?

That's okay. Hegel's audience was limited too. People will always read Plato and Nietzsche, and they will also read Derrida on Plato. At least some people. . .

Still on Derrida, how do you evaluate the success of "deconstruction" in America? Paradoxically, in Europe, where it was created, it occupies a much less central position.

I think that deconstruction is an American product. God only knows what it is, it is a very loosely used term. It really applies more to Paul de Man than to Derrida, but a de Manian literary criticism, as far as I know, simply does not exist. However, because we have a hundred thousand professors of English in America, it is part of the training in graduate school.

How would you define the difference between "deconstruction" and "textualism," the very successful term you coined in *Consequences of Pragmatism*?

I used textualism as a sort of lowest common denominator between de Man and Derrida, but it is not a term that should be pressed very hard. It is a way of doing with signs what used to be done with ideas.

What is the relationship between the notion of *text*, from which textualism is derived, and your concept of *narrative*?

Narrative means telling a story about something, like the world spirit, or Europe, man, the West, culture, freedom, class struggle. It is the story of some big thing like that, in which you can place your own story.

Then, the purpose of these stories is to allow culture a dialogue, more than communicating a comprehensive vision of the world.

I think that the purpose of constructing such narratives is to give sense to the author's existence. It is a way of relating himself or herself to the great men of the past. When you read Plato, Cervantes, or Dante, at some point you ask yourself what your connection is with them, and you tell yourself a story.

Is there an element of the monumental in what you are saying?

Sure. Because you have to think about great heroes, freedom, class struggle, as the great monuments of one's story.

In your last book you speak about "liberal utopia." What are you alluding to?

Nothing very new. I mean the ordinary notion of equality of opportunity, what Rawls describes in his book *A Theory of Justice,* the idea of a society in which the only reason for inequalities is that things would be even worse if they did not exist.

And what does the figure of the "ironic liberal" refer to?

If you speak about society in terms of this liberal utopia of equality of opportunity, and you don't have a philosophical backup such as the laws of history, or the decline of the West, or the age of nihilism, then you are in a position to be what I call an *ironist*. An ironist is someone who says that a liberal utopia isn't something that expresses the essence of human nature, the end of history, God's will, but is simply the best idea people have had about the object for which they work. Ironism, in this context, means something close to anti-foundationalism.

In the artistic avant garde, but also in the philosophical tradition from Socrates to Voltaire, the concept of irony is not simply a descriptive modality, but contains a subtle element of transgression.

In my use, it does not. The kind of irony I have in mind doesn't care about transgressing, because it doesn't think there is anything to transgress. It is just a sort of attitude, the way you feel about yourself, a form of life.

Where do you place existential themes such as death and anguish?

I don't believe that philosophy has one particular object. Some people spend a lot of time thinking about death, others about sex or money. I don't think that one of them is more philosophical by nature than any other.

I find your indifference to existentialism curious, and it brings me back to talking about your first approach to Heidegger. What were you looking for in Heidegger at the end of the fifties?

I was trying to understand what had happened after Hegel; the answer turned out to be Nietzsche. Hegel is such an overpowering figure that you wonder what there was left to do in philosophy after him. I think that I read Heidegger to find out what people who read Hegel were saying about him; I read Kierkegaard for the same reason.

You told me that your mother and father were old-time socialists. Was there any conflict in looking to Dewey instead of Marx?

Marxism always struck me as a perfectly reasonable criticism of capitalism imbued with a lot of philosophy. But compared to Hegel and Heidegger, Marx seemed to me third rate. Marx was good for economics. I had the same problem with Kolakowski. It seems very hard to read Marx without Lenin or Stalin.

How does the philosophy of science figure in your perspective?

Originally it meant empiricist epistemology; when Carnap and Reichenbach used this term, it was an attempt to repeat what the British empiricists had done in terms of sense perception. After Kuhn's *The Structure of Scientific Revolutions,* and the work of Feyerabend, the distinction between science and nonscience began to be blurred. It meant rethinking the nature of scientific endeavor in general.

Do you think that philosophy should assume a "critical" function with respect to science?

I don't see philosophy as criticizing anything. When people refer to philosophy as "critical," they seem say, "scientists or politicians use the vocabulary of some other philosopher, they shouldn't use that vocabulary, they should use mine!" When people say that philosophy criticizes science, or other areas of culture, all it comes down to is that it's criticizing the residues of past philosophies, as they appear in cultural practice.

I am having a hard time understanding how you tie together the liberal perspective and the idea of a philosophy totally estranged from social criticism.

We do not need philosophy for social criticism: we have economics, sociology, the novel, psychoanalysis, and many other ways to criticize society. Take the very powerful critic Foucault. His best work does not strike me as particularly philosophical. The most interesting parts of his work are the details about the culture of the insane asylums, of prisons, of hospitals. Foucault was also a great philosophical mind, but he made a social difference not as a philosopher, but as someone who looked at particular things harder than anybody else.

Then, what is philosophy? A testimony to the survival of a community of readers of philosophical texts?

I don't think one should ask that question. The reason I write philosophical books is all the other books I have read, and my reaction to those books. I react to some books and not others. Every once in a while you get an original poet, or sociologist, or philosopher, but it is a very bad idea for a discipline to say that it has a mission.

7

An Apology for Skepticism

Stanley Cavell

In many respects, Stanley Cavell seems the most European of contemporary American philosophers. His youthful oscillation between music and philosophy, his militancy among the ranks of "engaged" New York intellectuals in the immediate postwar period, his attention to historical genealogies of cultural phenomena, are all anomalies in the technical-argumentative hinterland of the philosophical community.

Curiously enough, it is this European-style background that has led him to question his origins, to rebuild a sort of phenomenology of the roots of that American culture which generated him, the son of central-European Jewish immigrants, born in the heart of the South, in Atlanta, Georgia, in 1926.

Alone among his Harvard colleagues, Stanley Cavell has embarked on a courageous recomposition of American thought, based on a concept of philosophy intended as a point of intersection, existentially very dense, between the various humanistic writings (literary, cinematographical, musical), that Cavell has produced as a critic and a scholar of aesthetics since his first book, *Must We Mean What We Say?* (1969).

Yet it would be a mistake to think of Cavell as a historian of ideas. As in the case of Michel Foucault, all his efforts at genealogical reconstruction would in fact be pointless if they were not in the service of a strong theoretical project coinciding with a complex revaluation of skepticism, a philosophical perspective that Cavell rehabilitates by interpreting it in a neo-Romantic key as anguish over the inevitably incomplete purview of knowledge.

Skepticism, for Cavell, is not a dimension of the disenchanted, the expression of a cultivated indifference to the univeralistic and totalizing seductions of knowledge. On the contrary, it represents the constant reproposing of self-examination, of the solitary existential interrogation of ultimate values: finitude, the fragility and tragedy of the human condition, seen in their irremediable disparity from transcendence.

More than neo-romantic, however, the atmosphere surrounding Cavell's thought is neo-transcendentalist. In the genealogy of skepticism, in fact, the first stage coincides with a "philosophical recovery" of American transcendentalism, generally and superficially considered a literary phenomenon. First among the postwar philosophers, Cavell lets emerge, against the historical backdrop of Puritan Massachusetts, two heroes of the American national saga: Ralph Waldo Emerson, and Henry David Thoreau, who remain today models for rebellious youth and for academic textual analysis.

Complex intellectual figures, devoted to public debate as much as to solipsistic meditation, inevitably suspended between Europe and the Orient, Emerson and Thoreau represent for Cavell an inalienable root of American culture that the "professionalization" of philosophy has unforgivably eliminated. The collection of essays entitled *The Senses of Walden* bears witness to a passion never really abandoned, that Cavell has experienced in different stages: from the first publication of *The Senses of Walden* (1972), entirely dedicated to the work of Thoreau, to two essays on Emerson, "Thinking of Emerson" (1979) and "An Emerson Mood" (1980).

But that is not all. Ahead of their time, Emerson and Thoreau embody a distinctly skeptical philosophical ideal, which consists in a sensibility for the quotidian sphere of the *ordinary*—the only aspect of transcendence we are allowed to touch; the perception of the infinite transfigured in the minute finitude of the quotidian. It is a concept at first romantic and then transcendental that Cavell finds articulated in the philosophy of ordinary language, developed in the twentieth century by Ludwig Wittgenstein and John Austin. Not by coincidence, Stanley Cavell was a student and collaborator of the latter during his first stay at Harvard University.

Cavell has concentrated his theoretical and genealogical effort on the itinerary that has led him from transcendentalism to the philosophy of ordinary language, as two of his principal works testify: *The Claim of Reason: Skepticism, Morality, and Tragedy* (1979), and *In Quest of the Ordinary: Lines of Skepticism and Romanticism* (1988).

According to Cavell, the hegemony of scientistic and epistemological analyticism, following in the footsteps of Carnap, Reichenbach, Hempel and the teachers of the Vienna Circle, has until now hindered the genuine reception of the English philosophy of ordinary language, especially the work of Austin and, above all, Ludwig Wittgenstein, whose writing cannot be reduced to or utilized in any "professional" form, to the neglect of its potential for metaphysical reflection.

In a recent series of lectures, published under the Emersonian title of *This New Yet Unapproachable America* in 1989, the intensity of Wittgenstein's philosophical gaze is defined as "the scene of illusion and loss," the expression of that fundamental oscillation between immanence and transcendence that skepticism not only reveals, but reproduces in the everyday practice of thought. In reflecting its fascination for the quotidian, writing becomes the source of an actuality that in itself contains the terms of eventuality, of the impetus toward its own ideal overcoming.

*

American culture has elaborated its own sense of the notion of "intellectual," on the one hand attributing to this figure a strong connotation of public engagement, and on the other denying it any organic status in the world of the university. The opposition between intellectual and scholar is the consequence. You are one of the few American philosophers to have felt the urge to resolve this problem, trying to provide some historical explanations. Do you see yourself not only as a professor, but as an intellectual as well?

The opposition between intellectual and scholar is one of the most deeply rooted in today's American culture, yet they are very difficult terms to use, partly because of the lack of tradition for either of them. What do these mean in America? I constantly ask myself. They're undefined for America, America is undefined. I don't mean there aren't great scholars in America. There are some great scholars. But there are no, or very few, nationally famous professors or intellectuals who speak for the country. It's hard to think, at the moment, of one individual who speaks from both sides, the scholarly and the intellectual, but just think of Hannah Arendt or Theodore Adorno, who both spent time in this country.

Are Emerson and Thoreau, the two heroes of transcendentalism whom you, for the first time, gave philosophical substance, intellectuals or scholars?

I constantly ask myself that. If an American is an intellectual, he or she more commonly would have to feel they are composing the autobiography of America when they write. They are not standing someplace else within a vast tradition and commenting on a scene that relates itself to the rest of the world. The effort of the American intellectual is not to relate himself to the world but to interrogate and discover himself.

Especially in the last few years, there has been a reevaluation of American intellectual history, focusing on the New York scene in the thirties, and the vibrant social commitment of its intelligentsia.

Everyone says there was a moment in New York in the thirties and forties when there was a set of intellectuals who had some apparent way of speaking for the culture at large. First of all, did it? And second, what kind of phenomenon was it in a sociological sense? It's a tiny glancing moment, but it had a tremendous influence on me when I was a graduate student, not knowing whether I wanted to be a musician or a philosopher. Yes, my undergraduate degree is in music and I was nothing but a musician at the university, when it all came apart. It wasn't what I wanted. I was born in Atlanta, Georgia, and as an undergraduate at Berkeley I was a student of Ernest Bloch. Then I came to New York and I went to the Julliard School of Music.

When was your future as a philosopher decided?

When I arrived in New York it was already clear that I was not going to be a musician. I did nothing but spend all day writing—reading Freud and writing, trying to take myself apart into all the original pieces, and put them all back together into some other form. And finally, from there, I studied philosophy. In the course of playing hooky from my university classes and my conservatory lessons, I was reading Freud and the *Partisan Review*, the main organ in New York in the thirties and forties for this little group of intellectuals. I found it inspiring: Lionel Trilling and the first writings on film by Robert Warshaw put me in a sort of ecstasy. And then there were writers like Saul Bellow and Isaac Rosenfeld, whom I admired immensely. There were other journals, too—New Criticism was at its apex.

What was the reason for your divorce from the *Partisan Review*?

I wanted these quarterlies to speak to one another. I never quite understood how New Criticism could be so wonderful about literature and the *Partisan Review* so promising about intellectualizing and theorizing the world, but somehow their writers could rarely if ever appear in one another's pages. On the whole, Lionel Trilling would have been one of the few voices that could easily appear in either place, and he was rather to one side of the hardest of the new critical writers. That's why I distanced myself from them. While discovering the concepts used by these writers was an ecstatic experience for me, they always seemed somewhat limited. They always stopped short. Whenever I wanted to hear something else or to find my own contribution, to find my own voice, the literary analysis stopped. It always theorized but it stopped theorizing in a moment that could not give one enough air to breathe. The intellectualization seemed to me always to borrow words—fascinating words—words I knew I didn't possess, and I had to go and find out about them. But it was as if I wasn't able to establish genealogies of meaning. The words were deemed important relative only to the moment in which they were being used. But I knew even then that these concepts were not derived as they were being used. I was trying to hear my own voice—to hear my own tunes as a composer—and I couldn't hear myself in this writing, but I couldn't hear anyone else hearing themselves in this writing either.

Going back to the distinction between scholar and intellectual, you conclude that the only true American intellectual movement has been a fire in a haystack, almost a joke of destiny in a culture that is not capable of developing "intellectuality" in the European sense.

You can't talk about this distinction if you don't talk about America as such. I think this distinction represents the country, and represents it in all its indefinability. Of course, I don't mean there aren't great scholars in America, of course there are. But institutionally, what's an American? Most of what Emerson says in his essay on the American scholar is that there aren't American scholars in the sense of a preexisting model. I say to myself, who is an American professor? what is an American university? and what do these terms mean? Who is a professor? Maybe nobody. That's how I begin asking myself whether there are these roles to match these social concepts that you're asking me about. As for "American scholars," we don't know anything about them, what they're going to look like. They could be anybody: a bank clerk, a robber, or a professor. You don't have to look like what you are. Everyone in America can be a pretender to some throne, which by the Constitution we are not allowed to have.

Do you think that the same discourse is also valid for the institutional structure of American universities, so different from European universities, because they are so remote from public life, anchored in a model of isolation closer to the medieval monastery than to an integrated organ of social life?

I think so. They're probably the best in the world as universities, but what are they, sociologically? politically? What is a professor in an American university? The truth is that the American myth is not to have models—especially in philosophy, where I never complied with the "technical framework" of analytic philosophy, which allows you to identify with a tradition and to use it. This is true not only for universities but for cities as well, which reconstruct themselves while they're still constituting themselves. So, it's an American way out to say that all we invented is all for the future.

Referring to New York, you have mentioned European intellectuals such as Adorno and Hannah Arendt. However, they represent one faction of the great European émigrés between the two wars, and, in particular, the half that American culture generally refused. The other side, in the field of philosophy, was constituted by the authors of the Vienna Circle, such as Rudolf Carnap, Hans Reichenbach, and Carl Hempel, who, on the contrary, had an incredible impact on the American continent, inaugurating analytic philosophy. Could it be that their success was determined precisely by the fact that they were not intellectuals but scholars?

I'm not sure that was the only reason, but it was certainly an important one. An American asks himself first, what profession or institution do I belong to? and being an intellectual is not a profession in America. So, Hannah Arendt was widely admired almost as soon as she came. *The Origins of Totalitarianism* appeared very shortly after that, and it was a very great success. But she was not taken as a model for what an American professor might be. The refugees provided a certain model of the intellectual life, but there was not, I think, the feeling that Americans were going to live that life, however much they could learn from somebody who did. Anyway, what happened to the European intellectual class in America was that we were saving their lives, and this rendered their models weak in our eyes. After all, who would have wanted to become a citizen of the Weimar Republic? What would have been the cost? That is the question to contemplate. Does this democracy produce and sustain an intellectual existence? It is the perennial question of American thinkers and writers, to the extent that they cannot identify themselves as professionals. If you can, then you don't have to ask the question any more.

And how does philosophy fit into the framework of the professional definition of a discipline?

In philosophy, a way to handle the matter in this country is to become a technical analytic philosopher. That is a recognizable profession, and it is the way that Dewey took, adopting the only technical apparatus to which a "professional legitimacy" was attached, and abandoning any historical visions of "philosophical" questions. To some extent, even before analytic philosophy, Dewey tried to dismantle the history of philosophy by not attending to it. In a sense, not attending to it is also a way of doing a kind of social good. Dewey was debunking rather than replacing philosophy, and in a way this was part of a great journalistic tradition in America—the tradition of the muckraker. Instead of finding that philosophy comes from the deepest of spiritual needs, which conflict with themselves, you find that it has its origin in social muck. It's not a matter of which of these is more reductive, it's what they reduce things to. If you reduce cultural aspirations to libido that's one thing; if you reduce it to class conflict it's something else. If you reduce it to radical spiritual dissatisfaction—insatiability—it's yet another thing. But if you reduce it to muck, it's bad behavior.

In this sense, the imposition of an exaggerated logical techni-calism could be the sign of American culture's fundamental un-certainty about its own significance.

Another way of putting it is that analytic philosophy in its technical-ities looks like a profession. You can justify to the neighbors why you do what you do if it is technical. The other feature is that you also must feel that you are contributing to some social good, and Dewey did that. It is the attempt to make thought creative for Americans. He said "practical" rather than "creative" but I think this is part of what he meant; he felt that being creative was an absolutely valuable thing to do. But would it have been practical and creative in his sense had he tried to accommodate the stream of history of philosophy that comes out of Frankfurt? My answer to that is no, it would not have felt that way to him, and even though anyone could say he began his life as a Hegelian, really the Hegel that Dewey uses consists of two or three moves. They are very important moves. They are moves that exist by trying to find the middle way of two extremes, but they are not moves that sense the spiritual negation—the mutual negation—of these extremes. So that to find a way out of the mutual negation is itself a kind of spiritual torture. In Dewey you don't have spiritual torture.

In the last twenty years, with the decline of pragmatism and the apogee of analytic philosophy, the disciplinary field of philoso-phy has been reduced to a reflection of a logico-epistemological type, excluding completely the "Continental" tradition of the

twentieth century, from historicism to phenomenology to existentialism.

The problem is always, ultimately, America itself. Now we come to what the differences in the professions are in America as opposed to other places, and how intellectual disciplines exist in such radical isolation from one another. Not even defined against one another, just in isolation from one another. That has terrible intellectual costs, but it also has intellectual virtues. The cost is professionalization and over-specialization, but it also has the virtues of a profession, namely knowing something very well. Professional progress, responsibility, the ability to be understood, of being a teacher and of explaining yourself to your fellow citizens, are all virtues. Why do you do what you do? You must have an answer to this. The answer can't be "Because I'm an intellectual," or "Because I'm an artist." When Howard Hawks was discovered by American universities he had to pretend he was a cowboy in order to make himself comprehensible. He couldn't let them know that he had a very good education. He wouldn't have been taken seriously as an American artist.

In this sense, do you consider yourself more a writer or a philosopher?

There's no question in my mind that my motivation, ever since I can remember, has been to write. In music, it was to write. When music fell apart for me, it's not exactly that I thought the writing I did was bad. I felt it wasn't anything I was saying, just something I had learned to do. The road that took me to philosophy was an attempt to discover a way to write that I could believe. First through Freud, through the *Partisan Review,* then through nineteenth-century American literature.

But do you really consider Freud a philosopher?

That's the problem. Are these things philosophy? Philosophy is in some ways the last place in the American landscape that you would look in order to learn to write. Yet, in a sense, to write your own words, to write your own inner voice, is philosophy. But the discipline most opposed to writing, and to life, is analytic philosophy. To oppose writing: I interpreted that opposition as an opposition to the human voice, which is where I come into philosophy. This is what my first essays are about—the suppression of the human voice in academic analytic philosophy. But, paradoxically, I felt nothing else was as promising as that same philosophy. The fastidiousness, the absolute desire to make every mark on the page have a meaning, which is also my prerogative, was first set forth by analytic philosophy. But it doesn't come out in its writing. So how can I have both?

Didn't you have moments when you thought that the two aspects were irreconcilable and that you should have abandoned philosophy as well?

I always had trouble even at school with this fact. In my literary classes, the few I had, I got myself entangled in philosophy. In my philosophy classes, I got entangled in writing and I was criticized— rewarded but criticized—from each side. For years I thought it wasn't going to happen, and I tried to leave philosophy, but there was no place to go outside philosophy. I mean, you can leave any place for America, but you can't leave America except to be a permanent emigrant. My father was already an immigrant. A very important fact to me was that he spoke no language naturally. A Polish Jew whose Polish was gone, whose Yiddish was frozen, and whose English was broken. And it was partly for that reason, I believe, that Austin was important to me, with his emphasis on the ordinary, the natural. To investigate natural language: exactly the thing my father lacked. I cite Austin because it was at the time he visited Harvard that I stopped trying to leave philosophy. I was rewarded for it, but I was still not convinced I was doing anything that was either philosophy or writing. It felt as though it was all just a kind of imitation.

There is a great sense of disorientation and disappointment in the narrative of your beginnings.

Yes, there's nothing but dissatisfaction in this early story. I define myself as a writer, but in philosophy the last thing you could say was that you wrote. Only in recent years have I actually said that what I'm doing is writing. But what's an American writer? An American writer is somebody who either can make a living at writing—an important fact—or who is a poet. For poets, a community exists.

They write for one another and they know it. Or, of course, you teach writing. But teaching writing has exactly nothing to do with what I have ever hoped to do as a writer. I never thought it was a part of what I would do.

Going back to Austin. When did you meet him?

He arrived at Harvard in 1955 to give a series of William James Lectures on "how to do things with words," that eventually came out as a book under the same title. He also gave a seminar on the same topic, which turned out to be his theory on speech acts. He hit me like a ton of bricks. It was as if a wall fell on me. I threw away a Ph.D. thesis that was pending and I talked to him for months when he was here. He gave his seminar, he gave public lectures, he had a faculty seminar that I was invited to, and his door was always open in the Harvard house that he lived in. As an Oxford tutor he was used to seeing students all the time. Americans are not used to going to see their professors. So anytime you wanted, you just went, and he was alone, and we'd talk. And so, I stopped asking how philosophy was relevant to me and began to feel that perhaps I had something to say in philosophy. The conversations confirmed my view that, whatever writing meant to me, it had to be philosophy— it had to thematize philosophy. So I tried to make a career out of these torments. Well, it's what one does.

A love for Austin is often accompanied by a passion for Witt- genstein. . .

I never had a chance to meet Wittgenstein. I tried reading him for the first time when the *Philosophical Investigations* were published in English in 1953. But it left me cold. In fact, it sounded like an unsystematic version of John Dewey. It's about context, it's about the absence of privacy, it's about the use of words, but—I thought at the time—devoid of any social pertinence. I even found its theory of language superficial. So I put it aside. Only after meeting Austin, and being completely absorbed in that, and after publishing the first thing I care about, the essay "Must We Mean What We Say?" did I get into Wittgenstein again. The experience of reading the *Investigations* at that stage was comparable to what had happened when I read Freud's lectures on psychoanalysis, while playing hooky from my composition lessons. I had the impression that *this person knows me*, that *this text knows me*.

If you had to think about a teacher, would you choose Austin or Wittgenstein?

When I reread Wittgenstein, it was a difficult moment in my relationship with Austin. Austin had already dissatisfied me, and I was ready for something else. Like Wittgenstein, Austin also refused philosophy, but I felt that he refused philosophy unphilosophically. He was extraordinarily kind to me, extraordinarily encouraging, but when pressed on why what he did was important he would answer, importance is not important; truth is. And I would reply, you can't just say importance is not important, because you are talking about importance when you ask what the context is, what tone of voice it is in which something is said. You are asking what is the importance of saying it. It was in this spirit that I was asking Austin about the importance of his work. He just shrugged. But when I came to the *Investigations*, I felt, here is a refusal of philosophy that *is* philosophy. This is the tone in which philosophy can refuse philosophy.

In the ranks of contemporary American thinkers, you are probably the only one to attribute to Emerson and to the transcendentalists of the mid–nineteenth century the role of philosophers. Is there a rapport between Emerson and the Austin-Wittgenstein axis?

By now I have digested both Austin and Wittgenstein, but I haven't yet fully digested Emerson. I mean, everything I would tell you about Emerson would just be Emerson at this stage, until I work myself through it. I am still not through with it. I came upon Emerson via Thoreau, America's first philosophical voice. I assigned Thoreau, not Emerson, to a group of visiting Europeans in the International Seminar created by Henry Kissinger in the early sixties. I ran the humanities section of the seminar. The important section was politics and economics, led by Kissinger, but there were always a few artists and writers and philosophers. We were away from home. We were like kids again. We all lived here without our families and it was like being in school again. Lasting friendships came from these meetings. You regressed. I assigned some of the major writers of the nineteenth and twentieth centuries. And then I thought, what about *Walden*? They'll be amused at least.

Walden is a key text in the curriculum of American high schools. Perhaps, even for you, there was a regression to adolescence. . .

I hadn't read it in twenty years, and when I read it again a wall fell. The entire edifice of everything I had been doing collapsed on top of me and I had to make my way out brick by brick. From that crisis, my book *The Senses of Walden* was born. It's an attempt to prove that, in American culture, writing and thinking happen simultaneously. That's when I knew it, though at first I couldn't believe it: *Walden* for me is a combination of Heidegger and Hölderlin. It's as if Thoreau, reincarnated in Hölderlin, were rewriting Heidegger, trying to answer him, combining the world of both—as if Thoreau were playing Hölderlin to his own Heidegger. First he says one thing, then he responds to this reflectively, and then he combines both things into one sentence. How can you possibly assign this thing in a high school? I said to all my intellectual friends, Have you read *Walden* recently? And no, of course they hadn't. They read it in high school, or the first year of college at the latest. A good book, worthy, very fine, they would say. Nothing against it, but it's not a part of any educated American's conversation, and certainly not part of any European's conversation. It's seen as a child's book, an adolescent's book, just like everybody thinks—or used to think—all great American books were.

If I'm not mistaken, this took place in the sixties, when the student movement had interpreted *Walden* as a compendium of "passive resistance" to institutions, a model of subversive but nonviolent anarchy, an ecological alternative to the consumer society.

I cannot deny that the sixties were important to my passion for Thoreau. I participated in the International Seminar in 1968, a year which won't be forgotten in history. Paris in '68 is more famous than America in '68, but it was a very important year for us—Martin Luther King, Robert Kennedy, the student movement. Nobody was really aware of how Thoreau's philosophy converged with the student movement, even if Martin Luther King was quoting him, and

I had had him in mind for a long time already. I approached Thoreau for reasons more profound and complicated than a simple convergence with the themes of the student movement, and he has become one of the major focuses of my reflection.

What relationship did you establish between Thoreau and Emerson at first?

The initial consequence of reading Thoreau was that, by comparison, Emerson was dead for me. I tried reading him because I was asked about him, but it all just seemed to be faded flowers and, I felt, hopeless. Nothing: no tune to it, no music. Or bad music, not my music. But again, like a good American, I read him because he was assigned to me. I accepted the assignment to read and talk on Emerson, but perhaps I had already preassigned myself this acceptance.

What role did European reflection play in your passion for transcendentalism? Emerson above all was an author profoundly loved by Europe, and as a philosopher he was perhaps appreciated more in Europe than in the United States. Think of Nietzsche, for example.

My admiration for Emerson was an admiration of something in Nietzsche, knowing Nietzsche's love for Emerson, and knowing that Thoreau would not exist but for Emerson. How was it that, at first, Emerson could not speak to me? Then, in the seventies, Harold Bloom and William Gass and I were asked to do a symposium together. I didn't want to say no to the assignment and so, as often in my life, I had to find out why I had already said yes to it. And the reason, immediately, turned out to be exactly the Nietzschean connection. It was then that I began to see a connection between Emerson and Nietzsche. Once I had made the connection, I began to draw ever closer to Emerson.

Then, it was drawing near by means of hermeneutic spirals?

In a certain sense, yes. But, once again, as an American I don't ask myself how Nietzsche makes Emerson thinkable but, on the contrary, what it is in Emerson that inspired Nietzsche's love, and allowed him to be Nietzsche—and there *is* something else. The depth of the connection between them is unknown. Everyone has to discover that for themselves. No matter how many people tell you the connection exists, you forget it, and you can't believe it, and not until you begin to have both voices in your ears do you recognize what a transfiguration of an Emerson sentence sounds like when Nietzsche rewrites it. But I've just gone through the third "Untimely Meditation," the one on Schopenhauer, and parts of *The Genealogy of Morals,* and one senses Emerson breathing in it. Emerson is retranscribed in Nietzsche. But it is as if Schoenberg orchestrated Brahms! It is still Schoenberg, it doesn't sound like anybody else, certainly not Brahms. The second sentence of *The Genealogy of Morals*—everybody reads that sentence—and the opening sentence of Emerson's essay on experience both ask the question: "Where do we find ourselves?" Now, the way I read Nietzsche is that he answers this question with another question: "How should we find ourselves, since we've never even looked at ourselves?" I think the answer to Emerson's question is to be found in Nietzsche's question. It doesn't matter at all if it can never be discovered that Nietzsche actually knew he was addressing Emerson's question. Of course, I don't dismiss the importance of investigating the connection empirically. But, in a philosophical sense, Nietzsche certainly was responding to Emerson, and that's what interests me most.

So far we have not spoken about the Thoreau-Emerson connection.

It is the same empathy. Thoreau says, I am the ancient Egyptian and Hindu philosopher. Now, philosophy in this sense is transhistorical. Or, at least, it gets transfigured throughout history. This is especially true in America, with the myth of the classless society. We don't know how people should look, so we have less difficulty in saying we can be the same as them.

Your attention is always on America, being American, and American culture. This certainly makes you somewhat eccentric in the panorama of American philosophy, in which no one recognizes a distinctly American line of continuity. What was the starting point of your interrogation, by which the familiar scenario dissolved into the history and mythology of the new continent?

My family never had the problems of the intellectual emigrant, because my father was unlettered. The fact that my father did not have a usable language and culture of his own did not deprive him of an intellectual perspective. It was a practical problem. But then you have also to include my mother, who was a concert pianist. How they got together is something else, because they both lived in the Jewish section of the same town, so everybody knew one another. But *why*, how this happened, is another story, and if I ever learned to be a good second-rate novelist, I would tell this story. My father had no native language left. My mother had perfect pitch in her musician's ear. And that is something that Austin meant directly to me, the exploration of natural language by means of perfect pitch. This has to be what all writing means to me. I saw it first in Austin, but that's what Emerson is for me. The Emersonian sentence is always a problem for any critic that looks at it. What are these sentences doing? Are they connected to one another? What's the topic sentence? That they are each of them a universe entails for me the investigation of the language to which this sentence is native. It could be any language, but the web that produces this sentence can only be investigated by perfect pitch. That's my fantasy; that's the myth of writing for me. Well, I mean, Frege says—and Wittgenstein quotes Frege—you can only understand a sentence in the context of a language. Well, I say, what language? What's a sentence and what's a language?

Is the idea of the perfect ear tied to a primitive sense of nature, unfastened by cultural contextuality? And is it tied in some way to your reading of skepticism?

Skepticism is the denial of the need to listen. It's the refusal of the ear. Skepticism denies that perfection is available through the human ear, through the human sensibility. This is what Wittgenstein calls the "sublimation" of our language, and he means sublime in the same sense that Kant did. It's as though we were on a slab of ice: on the one hand there is the smoothness of the surface, its perfection; on the other, our inability to walk on it. In one sense, conditions are perfect, but, for that reason, we as humans cannot belong. We are all too human. Skepticism as a search for the inhuman is a search for a means to the perfection of the ear, to the

extent that the ear is no longer required to listen. It is the denial
of having to hear.

**Is it possible to establish a relation between what you say about
the experience of imperfection and the perceptive experimentation of some artistic avant garde of the twentieth century?**

Yes, I have thought so from the first time I noticed this was
happening, as I read Wittgenstein. There I felt that the refusal of
the work was in itself a relation to its past, of a sort that I felt in
the avant-garde work that I knew. It was both an incorporation and
a refusal of its past, of the sort I saw going on in music, in theater,
and in painting. I would say in the novel as well, except that, for
Americans, the destruction of the novel by the novel had already
happened. (This is another question, of when things happened.
Things happened at different times in Europe than in America.)
Emerson begins in 1830; but think of what had already happened
in Europe in 1830. Hegel hadn't happened in America, Kant hadn't
happened in America, philosophy hadn't happened in America.
Thoreau graduated college in 1847. But what is 1848 in American
time? Is it a time of revolution, as in Europe? or is it the time when
Thoreau was looking for a job? In America the revolution occurred
in 1860—the Civil War.

**You say that the destruction of the novel through the novel had
already taken place in the United States. When?**

With Melville's *Moby Dick* and *The Confidence Man.*

Would you say the same about music?

When I was developing these thoughts initially, music was in a very
particular stage. The Schoenberg-Stravinsky issue was still tearing
people apart. And composers, in order to find their way, had to
compose theories first, or, as though they were first. It was difficult
to find an orientation at that time.

**What about composers like John Cage? Do you think he felt the
need to locate himself theoretically before writing?**

Sure. And Eliot Carter, and Milton Babbit. But I have been out of
the musical world for a long time. I am a musical tourist, and that's
the price I paid for having chosen writing.

You are originally from Georgia, and apart from a brief stay in New York you have always lived here in New England, two steps away from where Emerson, Thoreau, and the transcendentalists wrote. Is that by chance, or is it a choice?

It's a choice. New York is not really a place where the sort of work that I want to do gets done. Of course, there are a lot of brilliant people there; but, on the whole, it's a city of performance. What's immense and great about New York is its capacity for performance. But that's not me. I'm not looking for performance, so that even if it is a city that I love, I would never have chosen to live my life in New York. For an American, living and writing in New England is like breathing in the heart of history. It's very important to me that Emerson wrote "The Divinity School Address" a few blocks from here. Henry James went to school down the street. One can't think about America without having a theory of America. The reason I go over and over this is the difficulty of intellectual friendship in America, in the absence of intellectual institutions. Melville and Hawthorne had to walk all day long, one day, three weeks after *Moby Dick* appeared, for Hawthorne to say to Melville, "I like your book." At which point, so the story goes, Melville burst into tears. This is just an anecdote, but it explains some of the difficulty in writing being a public matter. If you are a member of intellectual society in France or Italy, you are born with your first three books written. The language writes them for you. Culture writes them for you.

You have a profound and consciously elaborated Jewish sensibility. The European Jewish tradition, with its emphasis on writing, proposes the "handing down" of culture. How do you reconcile this sense of tradition with your experience as an American, with your love for contingency and the ordinary, as defined by Wittgenstein and Austin?

Of all the times I've been asked about ordinary language, nobody has ever asked me this question before. It's so vast I don't quite know how to respond. But it's an extremely interesting question, and I'm fascinated to think about it. "Ordinary" has a philosophical negative built into it: the "ordinary" works, but it refuses philosophical technicality, it refuses the idea that there is a philosophical language, a special philosophical vocabulary. However, it does have political potential, in the sense that it doesn't postpone social justice to the future. And, finally, a religious accent. This is Emerson, and that's why I say he's a philosopher of the ordinary. It's as if I ask you, what's important about Christ, that he's transcendent or that he's human? I mention that because Kierkegaard is as authorizing a figure for me, as enabling a figure, in terms of my interest in the "ordinary" as any other single writer, because of his emphasis in *Fear and Trembling* on the sublime as resident in the pedestrian.

I asked you about your being Jewish and you answer me by talking about Christ and Kierkegaard!

To choose between Judaism and Christianity is, I suppose, still a live issue for me. I don't mean that I would convert to either. I grew up as a Jew and I believe in Martin Buber about these things. You don't have to convert to being a Jew. You do have to convert to being a Christian. This also sounds like Kierkegaard, so perhaps I'm still avoiding you. Let me see if I can do better. For me to say that the figure of Christ is an obsessive figure for a Jewish intellectual is hardly news. I went to Jerusalem three years ago for the first time in order to really see for myself if there is such a thing as an everyday Jewish life apart from religion or apart from living in Israel. Is it some form of nostalgia for me, or piety, or what? At the same time, I made Thoreau write a scripture that is as much old testament, and I made Emerson into the philosopher of immigrancy.

From Christ, once again, to Emerson. . .

Yes, because he is the philosopher who contradicts Heidegger's effort to dwell by saying that you have to leave. Abandonment is for me the first door. You abandon the word you write, the house you live in, your father and mother, your sister and brother. You have to leave when the kingdom of heaven calls you. But what's the kingdom of heaven? Emerson pictures it as writing, which in turn he will abandon only for thinking. So, in this sense of abandoning things and moving on, Emerson is a Jew, Thoreau is a Jew, and I'm a Jew. Or at least I would like to become one.

8

Nietzsche or Aristotle?

Alasdair MacIntyre

Suspended between reminiscences of a past with very ancient roots, sunk deep into the Scottish world of celtic tradition, and the global perspective of American pluralism, Alasdair MacIntyre has enriched contemporary moral debate to an unparalleled extent. Moving with a totally new agility between the meshes of historicism, his discourse points to the circumscription of a neo-Thomist horizon, understood not as a moment of categorical refoundation but, on the contrary, as the point of arrival of the "ethics of virtue," a line of secular reflection that traverses all of classical Greece and reaches full systematization in the thought of Aristotle.

Born in Glasgow, Scotland, in 1929, MacIntyre had to await immersion in the American melting pot, at the age of forty, before imposing some order on the crucible of traditions in which he was forged. A classicist reeducated by analytic philosophy, he spent these first forty years trying to unravel the strands of an intellectual ball of twine including an Anglo-Saxon liberalist heritage, a self-determined Marxist faith, and, finally, a Christian urgency disavowed and rehabilitated in various versions, as testified to by his book *Marxism and Christianity* (1982).

The confrontation with analytic philosophy is the one that has perhaps left the fewest traces on the body of MacIntyre's thought. He criticizes the thematic limitation, the focusing on logical detail and, most of all, the systematic dichotomy between method and historical perspective in this tradition, to which England has contributed with ordinary language philosophy, initiated by John Austin and Ludwig Wittgenstein and continued by the authors of the Oxford-Cambridge school.

In precisely this respect, the encounter with Marxism represented a point of crucial transformation that accompanied the Scottish philosopher during his solitary transatlantic flight. It was Marxism that resolved one of his foremost anxieties, connected to that sort of "innatism" that the Anglo-Saxon world tends to attribute to liberalistic thought. Through the lens of Marxist historicism, liberalism revealed itself to MacIntyre in its "ideological projectuality," based on the impoverishment of the traditional community and, consequently, on the progressive dissolution of the human links in the network of cultural and social relationships.

It was only a short step from the historicization of liberalism to a comprehensive rethinking of the entire Enlightenment project. Starting in 1966 with *A Brief History of Ethics,* this new phase of MacIntyre's thought was followed with the publication of the work on moral theory, *After Virtue* (1981), that was greeted with considerable international acclaim.

In contrast with the universalism of moral assumptions on which Enlightenment rationalism was nourished, a plurality of theses flourished in the post-Enlightenment epoch—Kantian, utilitarian, contractualist—revealing the fundamental bankruptcy of the ethics of Aufklärung, a defeat that projects its effects into the twentieth-century incapacity to appeal to any moral code whatever. Having denied morality its historical roots and its social context, the Enlightenment must bear the burden of having pushed Western culture from modernity toward Nietzsche: that is, toward the systematic refusal of morality expressed in the extremes of genius and nihilism.

But what are the reasons for the disastrous failure of the Enlightenment project? According to MacIntyre, the failure must be ascribed to the misunderstanding that late Renaissance and Baroque culture, long before the Enlightenment, perpetrated on the Greek tradition of "virtue," born during the transition from the most ancient forms of community to the Athenian polis of the fifth century B.C.

This transition, which has its principal reference points in Socrates, in Plato, and, above all, in Aristotle, frames morality in a specific historical context; that is, in the custom and the dynamic of communication internal to a specific community. Virtue is not a universal and metahistorical category, but a pluralist and shared value.

The line of classical thought followed by MacIntyre defines the pluralist concept of virtue according to at least three meanings. First, virtues represent qualities of mind and of character, to which are linked the success of a series of typically human activities, such as art, science, and agriculture. Second, without virtue the individual is prevented from attaining an "ordered" life. And, third, it is only thanks to these models of moral excellence that the individual is able to contribute to the ultimate value, the construction of the public good.

Articulated by Aristotle in an incomparable political and metaphysical network, into which MacIntyre delves deeply in his two most recent books, *Whose Justice? Which Rationality?* (1988) and *Three Rival Versions of Moral Equity: Encyclopedia, Genealogy and Tradition* (1990), the tradition of virtues survives through the existentially dense contribution of Augustinian subjectivism and flows on into Thomas Aquinas.

To the question "Nietzsche or Aristotle?" with which *After Virtue* concluded in 1981, the answer today is all too clear: Aristotle; including along with that ancient peripatetic philosopher and Saint Thomas, two other unexpected disciples—the master of Mediterranean historicism, Giambattista Vico, and the most recent voice of Atlantic neo-historicism, R. G. Collingwood.

     *

Not only are you one of the last European philosophers to have left the Old World for the New, but you are also one of the most enigmatic, because at the basis of this choice are neither racial nor political considerations. If you had to describe, in a few words, the cultural and existential baggage you carried with you on your first crossing, what would you include?

Long before I was old enough to study philosophy I had the philosophical good fortune to be educated in two antagonistic systems of belief and attitude. On the one hand, my early imagination was engrossed by a Gaelic oral culture of farmers and fishermen, poets and storytellers, a culture that was in large part already lost, but to which some of the older people I knew still belonged with part of themselves. What mattered in this culture were particular loyalties and ties to kinship and land. To be just was to play one's assigned role in the life of one's local community. Each person's identity derived from the person's place in their community and in the conflicts and arguments that constituted its ongoing (or by the time of my childhood no longer ongoing) history. Its concepts were conveyed through its histories. On the other hand, I was taught by other older people that learning to speak or to read Gaelic was an idle, antiquarian pastime, a waste of time for someone whose education was designed to enable him to pass those examinations that are the threshold of bourgeois life in the modern world.

What were your perceptions of the "modern world" during a youth spent among these contrasting cultural realities?

The modern world was a culture of theories rather than stories. It also presented itself as the milieu of what purported to be "morality" as such; its claims upon us were allegedly not those of some particular social group, but those of universal rational humanity. So, part of my mind was occupied by stories about Saint Columba, Brian Boru, and Ian Lom, and part by inchoate theoretical ideas, which I did not as yet know derived from the liberalism of Kant and Mill.

Was it philosophy that suggested the way to reconcile these contrasting worlds?

Philosophy taught me the importance of not holding contradictory beliefs, partly by reading Plato and partly by coming across the proof, originally discovered by Thomas of Erfurt and then rediscovered by the pragmatist C. I. Lewis, that if you assert a contradiction, you are thereby committed to asserting anything whatsoever. So every contradiction within one's belief is a potential source of disaster. Yet in the same period in which I became aware of the importance of coherence and consistency in belief, the incoherence of my own mind was growing rather than diminishing. My school and undergraduate studies were in Latin and Greek—literature, philosophy, and history—and I became aware of the radical difference not only between classical Greek culture and liberal modernity, but also between the ancient Greeks and Irish tradition.

At that moment of your development, who were your guiding figures?

I began to read George Thomson, a professor of Greek first at Galway and then at Birmingham and a member of the Executive Committee of the British Communist Party. He played a part, I believe, in my joining the Communist Party for a short time. In 1941, he published "Aeschylus and Athens," which came after a history of Greek philosophy up to Plato written in Irish, entitled *Tosnù na Feallsùnachta,* as well as the translation of some Platonic dialogues into Irish. It was through thinking about the problems of translation involved in rendering Greek philosophy into modern languages as different as English and Irish that I had my first inklings of two truths: that different languages as used by different societies may embody different and rival conceptual schemes, and that translation from one such language to some other such language may not always be possible. There are cultures and languages-in-use that one can only inhabit by learning how to live in them as a native does. And there are theories framed in different languages-in-use whose incommensurability arises from their partial untranslatability. These were thoughts that I only developed fully some thirty-five years later in *Relativism, Power and Philosophy* and in *Whose Justice? Which Rationality?*

From what you say, one might suggest it was a matter of "hermeneutic glimmers": of intuition about the incommensurability and untranslatability of language, tied to the Continental tradition stretching from German Romanticism to Heidegger and Gadamer.

Yes, that's true, though at the time I didn't know much about hermeneutics. The reading that first my undergraduate, and then my graduate studies required of me only accentuated the incoherence of my beliefs. I read Aquinas as well as Aristotle. Sometimes I would find myself thinking about justice in an Aristotelian or Thomistic way, sometimes in a modern liberal way, without recognizing the full extent of my own incoherence. No wonder I found it increasingly difficult to discover adequate rational grounds for the belief in Christianity that I thought I had, and that faith came to look like arbitrariness.

In what sense was Christianity the disruptive element in all your contradictions?

For a time, I tried to fence off the area of religious belief and practice from the rest of my life, by treating it as a *sui generis* form of life, with its own standards internal to it, and by blending a particular interpretation of Wittgenstein's notion of a "form of life" with Karl Barth's theology. But I soon recognized that the claims embodied in the uses of religious language and practice are in crucial ways inseparable from a variety of nonreligious metaphysical, scientific, and moral claims, a conclusion I reached when reading Hans Urs von Balthasar's criticism of Barth. When I came to reject this strange philosophical mixture of a misunderstood Wittgenstein and an all-too-well understood Barth, I mistakenly rejected the Christian religion along with it. But parts of Thomism survived in my thought from those times, together with some more adequate reflections on Wittgenstein.

Your account of your development is saturated with existential inquietude. It is not clear to me how much of this is due to the friction between the ancient celtic narrative tradition and the modern, Anglo-Saxon utilitarian tradition, and how much to the imposing religious presence.

When I look back on my asserted beliefs in that period, I see my thinking as having been a clumsily patched together collection of fragments. And for years this vision was felt as a very disquieting one. Nonetheless, I was able to effect a reconciliation. The history of late-nineteenth-century physics and the problems that Maxwell and Boltzman faced when confronted by inconsistencies they could not know how to remove, convinced me that a premature regimentation of one's thought in the interest of total consistency may well lead to the rejection of important truths. However, I do remember my formation as being immersed in a painful state of mind, simultaneously drawn in a number of directions intellectually.

I imagine that this sense of disorientation was further exacerbated by the emergence of Marxism, to which tradition you were connected for a long time.

Certainly Marxism added another dimension of complexity. But it also represented a turning point. It was in thinking about Marxism that I began the work of resolving the conflicts in which I was trapped. Even if Marxist characterizations of advanced capitalism are inadequate, the Marxist understanding of liberalism as ideological, as a deceiving and self-deceiving mask for certain social interests, remains compelling. Liberalism in the name of freedom imposes a certain kind of unacknowledged domination, and one which in the long run tends to dissolve traditional human ties and to impoverish social and cultural relationships. Liberalism, while imposing through state power regimes that declare everyone free to pursue whatever they take to be their own good, deprives most people of the possibility of understanding their lives as a quest for the discovery and achievement of the good, especially by the way in which it attempts to discredit those traditional forms of human community within which this project has to be embodied.

The first result of your encounter with Marxism was therefore the refusal and criticism of liberalism in all its versions.

Yes, including the liberalism of contemporary American and English conservatives, as well as that of American and European radicals, and even the liberalism of the self-proclaimed liberals. Furthermore, it was Marxism which convinced me that every morality including that of modern liberalism, however universal its claims, is the morality of some particular social group, embodied and lived out in the life and history of that group. Indeed, a morality has no existence except in its actual and possible social embodiments, and what it amounts to is what it does or can amount to in its socially embodied forms. So that to study any morality by first abstracting its principles and then studying these in isolation from the social practice informed by them is necessarily to misunderstand them. Yet this is how almost all modern moral philosophy proceeds.

On this issue you are still, if not a Marxist, a materialist.

No. Because if I had gone on being a Marxist this lesson would not have been of much use to me. For Marxism is not just an inadequate, but a largely inept, instrument for social analysis. Most happily for me, when I was a student in London I met the anthropologist Franz Steiner, who pointed me toward ways of understanding moralities that avoided both the reductionism of presenting morality as a mere secondary expression of something else, and the abstractionism that detaches principles from socially embodied practice. Rival forms of such practice are in contention, a contention which is neither only a rational debate between rival principles nor a clash of rival social structures, but always inseparably both.

What is the role of dialogue in this contention? One of the errors of Marxism has often been its tendency to "canonize" and to dry up forms of social debate.

Personally, from the history of Marxism I learned how important it is for any theory to be formulated so that it is maximally open to the possibility of refutation. Only later on I realized that I could have learned the same lesson from a critic of Marxism such as Karl Popper, or from a pragmatist like Charles Peirce. If a standpoint is not able to be shown, by its own standards, to be discordant with reality, it cannot be shown to be concordant either. It becomes a scheme of thought within which those who give it their allegiance become imprisoned and also protected from the realities about which their beliefs were originally formulated.

Until now you have described the development of your thought in a negative key, trying to retrace the theoretical lines from which you have progressively detached yourself. What was the turning point toward the *pars construens* of your identity as a thinker? Your emigration to the United States, perhaps?

During the first twenty years of my philosophical career—from 1951 to 1971 when I had just emigrated to the United States—a good deal of what I did and thought was in the style of analytic philosophy. Analytic philosophy's strengths and weaknesses both derive from its exclusive focus on a rigorous treatment of detail, one that results in a piecemeal approach to philosophy, isolable problem by isolable problem. Its literary genres are the professional journal article and the short monograph.

In effect, at least since your book *After Virtue,* you have concentrated on restoring political legitimacy to the so-called great questions. How did these efforts contrast with those of the analytical establishment?

What analytic philosophy gains in clarity and rigor, it loses in being unable to provide decisive answers to substantive philosophical questions. It enables us—at least it enabled me—to rule out certain possibilities. But while it can identify, for each alternative view that remains, what commitments one will be making by way of entailments and presuppositions, it is not capable in itself of producing any reason for asserting any one thing over any other. When analytic philosophers do reach substantive conclusions, as they often do, those conclusions only derive in part from analytic philosophy. There is always some other agenda in the background, sometimes concealed, sometimes obvious. In moral philosophy it is usually a liberal political agenda.

Do you believe you have complete control of the "ideological" net that governs your thought?

It was in the latter part of my analytic stage, around the mid-sixties, that I developed a new agenda. I had come to recognize that a second weakness of analytic philosophy was the extent of the divorce between its inquiries and the study of the history of philosophy, and that analytic philosophy, and more especially its moral philosophy, could only itself be adequately understood if placed in historical context and thus understood as the intelligible outcome of extended argument and debate. So I wrote *A Short History of Ethics*, a book from whose errors I learned a lot.

What kinds of errors are you thinking about?

First of all, a recurring lack of continuity at certain points in the narrative. There is an account of the development of a distinctively Greek debate about ethics, an account of the development of a very different set of distinctive Christian lines of thought, and an account of the variety of argumentative encounters and rival conclusions that emerged from Enlightenment and post-Enlightenment moral philosophy. But what goes unremarked are the discontinuities at the points of transition from each one of these to the next. The fundamental shifts in central concepts and in basic principles are reported, but they appear as pure facts, unscrutinized and not at all understood.

The error, then, was not having individuated the value of certain discontinuities or epistemological *coupures* in the historical development of moral philosophy—a subject which seems to me to be directly in tune with contemporary debate on both sides of the Atlantic, from Thomas S. Kuhn to Michel Foucault.

Up to that point I had at least tried to present each phase in the history of ethics as the expression of the rational moral claims of some specific type of society. In that book I decided to counterpose two forms of moral utterance: on the one hand, the morality of those who use morality to express their membership in some particular type of society; on the other, the morality of those who use it to express their individuality, or social diversity. In a genuine morality it is the rules that have authority, not the individuals. The notion of choosing one's own morality makes no sense. What *does* make sense is the much more radical notion of choosing to displace and overcome morality. So *A Short History of Ethics* should perhaps have ended by giving Nietzsche the final word, instead of leaving him behind two chapters earlier.

I presume you are referring to the mature Nietzsche, author of *Beyond Good and Evil* and hero of the systematic overcoming of any value, the anarchic and individualistic Übermensch.

Nietzsche occupies this position insofar as he represents the ultimate answer to the systematic inconclusiveness and irreconcilable disagreements that were the outcome of Enlightenment and post-Enlightenment moral philosophy. The Enlightenment's central project had been to identify a set of moral rules, equally compelling to all rational persons. That project had failed and its heirs were a number of rival standpoints, Kantian, utilitarian, contractualist, and various blends of these, whose disagreements multiplied in such a way that twentieth-century culture has been deprived of any widely shared, rational morality, but has inherited instead an amalgam of fragments from past moral attitudes and theories. From a methodological point of view, it is today clear to me that while I was writing *A Short History of Ethics* I should have taken as a central standpoint what I learned from R. G. Collingwood: that morality is an essentially historical subject matter and that philosophical inquiry, in ethics as elsewhere, is defective insofar as it is not historical.

What do you mean by saying that morality is "an essentially historical subject matter"? Is it not possible that behind Collingwood and Marx, *lector in fabula,* peeps out Giambattista Vico?

Vico reminded us of what the Enlightenment had forgotten, that rational inquiry, whether about morality or about anything else, continues the work of, and remains rooted in, prerational myth and metaphor. Such inquiry does not begin from Cartesian first principles, but from some contingent historical starting point, some occasion that astonishes sufficiently to raise questions, to elicit rival answers and, hence, to lead on to contending argument. Such arguments, when developed systematically through time, become a salient feature of the social relationships they inform and to which they give expression. Prerational cultures of story telling are transformed into rational societies in which the stories are first put into question and then partially developed by theories, which are themselves in turn put to the question.

History would then coincide with pure cultural and narrative tradition. It is difficult to maintain that this argument does not entail a historicist conception of history.

To understand some particular philosophical position requires being able to locate it within such a tradition, always in relation to its successors. It is insofar as it transcends the limitations and corrects the mistakes of those predecessors, and insofar as it opens up new possibilities for those successors, that it achieves rational justification. It is insofar as it fails in these tasks that it fails as a philosophical theory. So the best theory, that to which we owe our rational allegiance, in moral philosophy as elsewhere, is always the best theory to be developed so far within the particular tradition in which we find ourselves at work.

However, from this point on it is easy to slide into a form of absolute relativism.

It can happen that a tradition of moral thought and practice fails to flourish. Its resources may not be adequate to solve the problems that are crucial to its rational inquiries. Its internal or external conflicts may undermine those agreements which made collaborative debate and inquiry possible. And its dissolution or rejection may leave a society without adequate resources for reconstructing its morality, while making the need for such reconstruction painfully evident.

And is this the case of the European Enlightenment at the end of the eighteenth century?

Precisely. In *After Virtue* I argued that the failure of the Enlightenment project is best understood as a sequel to the wrong-headed rejection, in the sixteenth and seventeenth centuries, of what I called "the tradition of the virtues." That tradition had its birth first in the transition from older forms of Greek community to the fifth-century Athenian polis, and then in the criticism and construction of a theory and practice of the virtues in which Socrates, Plato, and Aristotle are the key names. It is a tradition with a shared core conception of virtues. Virtues are those qualities of mind and character without which the goods internal to such human practices as those of the arts and the sciences and such productive activities as those of farming, fishing, and architecture cannot be achieved. Second, virtues are those qualities without which an individual cannot achieve that life, ordered in terms of those goods, which is best for her or him to achieve; and third, those qualities without which a community cannot flourish, and there can be no adequate conception of overall human good.

From a textual point of view, your stand on the recovery of "virtues," as opposed to the universalistic idea of "a virtue," in the singular, is anchored in the philosophy of Aristotle.

True. This complex conception of virtues received its classical statement from Aristotle in a form that requires not only the justification of the central theses of his political and moral philosophy, but also that of the metaphysics which those theses presuppose. This latter connection between virtue and metaphysics I had not understood when I wrote *After Virtue*. What I *had* recognized was that the failure of the Enlightenment project left open two alternatives: to reconstruct the moral theory and communal practice of Aristotelianism in whatever version would provide the best theory so far, explaining the failure of the Enlightenment as part of the aftermath of the breakdown of a tradition; or, instead, to understand the failure of the Enlightenment as a symptom of the impossibility of discovering any rational justification for morality as hitherto understood, a sign of the truth of Nietzsche's diagnosis. So the choice posed by *After Virtue* was: Aristotle or Nietzsche?

Why not Nietzsche?

For two reasons. One concerns Nietzsche and the spelling out in detail of his genealogical project by recent followers such as Michel Foucault and Gilles Deleuze. What they have quite unintentionally put in question is the possibility of making that project sufficiently intelligible in its own terms. The outcome of the unmasking of others by the genealogist seems to me to have been in the end the self-unmasking of the genealogists. A second reason for rejecting Nietzsche is an Aristotelian one. It reflects both a discovery that the narrative of my own uneven intellectual and moral development could only be both intelligibly and truthfully written in Aristotelian terms, and a recognition that in those medieval debates that reconstituted the Aristotelian tradition in Islamic, Jewish, and Christian milieus, Aristotelianism as a political and moral philosophy had both progressed by its own standards and withstood external criticism. It finally emerged in its Thomistic version as a more adequate account of the human good, of virtues, and of rules, than any other I have encountered.

Hence you try to reconcile two historically contrasting lines of thought: on one side, the historicist hypothesis, and on the other, the Aristotelian categorical instance. Your version of historicism emphasizes the idea that theories can be elaborated and criticized only in the context of specific historical-cultural traditions. Aristotelianism, in contrast, proceeds on the supposition that things are universally "based," and it does not start from the historical context of a specific tradition.

The claims made from within all well-developed traditions of inquiry on behalf of their own best philosophical, moral, and scientific theories are indeed generally claims to truth, claims about what anyone in any tradition must recognize if those claims are to be counted as genuine knowledge. The activities of inquiry themselves presuppose a strong and substantive conception of truth. And even if it is inescapable that the relationship between truth and rationality is problematic, it does not seem to me to be peculiarly a problem for Aristotelianism. One reason why some have thought there is an insuperable difficulty here is that they have understood that if any set of assertions or theory claims truth, then it must be possible to compare the merits of that claim with the merits of rival claims to truth made on behalf of incompatible sets of assertions or theories about the same subject matter. But if there are no neutral standards of rational justification independent of tradition, so that rival theories stemming from different traditions are each evaluated by reference to the standards internal to its own tradition, then it seems impossible to provide the requisite kind of comparison. Such rival theories will be incommensurable. Hence any historicism that relativizes rational justification to the context of particular traditions of inquiry has seemed incompatible with any standpoint, such as that of Aristotelianism, which asserts the truth of its conclusions.

And how do you counterattack this apparently flawless argument?

As I argued in *Whose Justice? Which Rationality?* the mistake is to suppose that if two or more rival bodies of theory have satisfied a condition of being formulated so as to be maximally open to refutation, each by the best standards available within its own tradition, then it is always possible that one of those rivals succeeds by its own standards in meeting all the critical challenges offered to it, while the other or others fail. That they fail by the standards of their own tradition does not make this any less a failure in achieving rational justification. It is in these terms that Aristotelianism failed with respect to key parts of its physics and biology, but succeeded in vindicating itself rationally as metaphysics, as politics and morals, and as a theory of inquiry. If this is so, then Aristotelianism has been shown in at least these areas to be not only the best theory so far, but the best theory so far about what makes a particular theory the best one. At this point, it is rational to proceed in philosophy as an Aristotelian, until and unless reasons are provided for doing otherwise.

I think you are the only one on the contemporary philosophical scene, and most of all on this side of the Atlantic, to repropose Aristotelianism as an epistemological perspective. How does it feel to be in this unique position?

Let's begin with our disagreements. Unlike Davidson, I hold that there are rival and alternative conceptual schemes, in some respect untranslatable into each other, and that alternative and rival conceptions of rationality are at home in different conceptual schemes. Unlike Rorty, I believe that there are strong and substantive conceptions of truth and rational justification—Aristotelian and Thomistic conceptions—that remain unscathed by his critique of epistemological foundationalism. From Gadamer I have learned a great deal about intellectual and moral tradition. I am very close to all in Gadamer that comes from Aristotle; that which comes from Heidegger I reject. I think that Heidegger was not at all in error when he discerned a close relationship between his own views and the philosophical politics of National Socialism. Although Lukács's critique of Heidegger was deformed by the crudities of his conformity to Stalinism, in his central contentions he was right.

Then even in this you assume a Marxist voice.

An Aristotelian critique of contemporary society has to recognize that the costs of economic development are generally paid by those least able to afford them; the benefits are appropriated in a way that has no regard to one's merits. At the same time, large-scale politics has become barren. Attempts to reform the political systems of modernity from within are always transformed into collaborations with them. Attempts to overthrow them always degenerate into terrorism or quasi terrorism. What is not thus barren is the politics involved in constructing and sustaining small-scale local communities, at the level of the family, the neighborhood, the workplace, the parish, the school, or clinic, communities within which the needs of the hungry and the homeless can be met. I am not a communitarian. I do not believe in ideals or forms of community as a nostrum for contemporary social ills. I give my political loyalty to no program.

Some critics suspect that your more recent philosophical positions conceal a reassertion of Christianity, that they are a new version of Catholic theology. Is there a basis of truth in all this?

It is false, both biographically and with respect to the structure of my beliefs. What I now believe philosophically I came to believe very largely before I reacknowledged the truth of Catholic Christianity. And I was only able to respond to the teachings of the

Church because I had already learned from Aristotelianism both the nature of the mistakes involved in my earlier rejection of Christianity, and how to understand aright the relation of philosophical argument to theological inquiry. My philosophy, like that of many other Aristotelians, is theistic; but it is as secular in its content as any other.

Your training and intellectual growth, as well as your present philosophical views seem to be solidly anchored in a European hinterland, tied to the age-old traditions and values of the Continent. Your love for classicism, your "hermeneutical" approach to tradition, your experience of the old celtic oral tradition handed down for hundreds of generations: what do those things have to do with the "impermeability" and the postmodernism of this country? Has your American naturalization involved a rupture with the past?

On the contrary, one of the great advantages of North America is that it is a place where different cultures meet and different histories intersect. It is the place where, in perspectives afforded by a variety of European pasts, of African and Asian pasts, and of course of native American ones, the conflicts between tradition and liberal modernity have had to be recognized as inescapable. The issues in moral philosophy that I am most concerned with necessarily have a kind of importance for the cultures of North America that they are not always accorded elsewhere. I have learned a good deal about the importance they have only because of living and working here.

9

Paradigms of Scientific Evolution

Thomas S. Kuhn

When Thomas S. Kuhn crossed the Atlantic to take the word to the International Colloquium on the Philosophy of Science in Bedford College in London, he never imagined that his intervention would provoke such a storm of controversy. Only three years had passed since 1962, the date of the first edition of *The Structure of Scientific Revolutions;* and it would be five more years before Kuhn, upset by the misunderstandings and the improper "uses" of his theories, would decide to prepare a postscript in response to his critics.

Published in the same *International Encyclopedia of Unified Sciences* that served as the editorial outlet of the Vienna Circle and its proselytes, Kuhn's book played the role of the Trojan Horse within the walls of positivism. It was a role that clearly reflected his *querelle* with the positivist residue present in Karl Popper's theory of falsifiability, inaugurated at the London Colloquium in 1965 and destined to remain, in Europe and in America, the central theme in the philosophy-of-science debate for the next fifteen years.

Born in Ohio in 1922, the young Kuhn adopted the Harvard campus as his new home. Apart from a temporary move to Princeton, Cambridge has remained his home ever since, and he currently teaches at the Massachusetts Institute of Technology.

In the immediate postwar period, he had not yet finished his doctoral thesis in physics when science began to reveal itself in a new historical perspective, undermining the attractions of the purely experimental approach. *The Copernican Revolution; Planetary*

Astronomy in Western Thought appeared in 1957; but it was not until the subsequent work, *The Structure of Scientific Revolutions,* that the historicist perspective would assume the force of a genuine epistemological thesis.

Kuhn's radical opposition to the positivist picture rotates on the notion of "scientific paradigm," indispensable to the comprehension of the evaluative parabola of science. Scientific activity, in fact, is distinguished by the succession of two types of phases: those of "normal science" and those of "revolutionary rupture."

The establishment of the first, "normal" phase depends on the gradual imposition of a theoretical system through the ever-increasing consensus of a community. From a preparadigmatic period, characterized by the chaotic accumulation of facts, scientific practice normalizes itself around the institution of a new "paradigm," which represents a normative mixture of theory and method—an amalgamation combining a spectrum of theoretical postulates, a precise vision of the world and of the modes of transmission of the contents of science, not to mention a series of research techniques. During this "normal" phase, the function of the scientist is limited to the "solution of a puzzle": that is, to the solution of problems whose theoretical horizon is guaranteed by the paradigm.

However, at a certain point the compactness of the paradigm begins to crack, and the phase of "normal" science turns into a phase of "revolutionary rupture." During this period of crisis, the method, the techniques, and the theoretical assumptions of the paradigm are put in question. Metaphysical questions are raised, and the entire net of epistemological values gradually transforms itself, until a new phase of normality is installed. The history of science is studded with such examples: the transition from the Aristotelian system to the Galilean, and from the Ptolemaic to the Christian in astronomy, and the passage from phlogistic chemistry to the chemistry of Lavoisier, to name only the most renowned instances.

According to Kuhn, the wellspring of scientific evolution is represented by discontinuity rather than continuity. And it is a matter of radical discontinuity, that precludes the possibility of communication between the new and the surpassed paradigms. In different paradigms, according to Kuhn, the same words "signify" different things; so different, in fact, that the paradigms are to be considered reciprocally "incommensurable."

This notion of incommensurability is at the center of the thesis that, starting with the publication of *The Structure of Scientific Revolutions,* and even more so after the Colloquium in London, placed Kuhn at the forefront of the opposition to neo-positivism and every form of thought based on it, including Popper's falsificationism. For Kuhn, there is no single, universal scientific method: researchers cannot compare their results with those of the universal "protocols" of observation, as the neo-positivists had thought, nor with any Popperian "base-assertions" available at any point in history. There is no absolute truth that constitutes the goal toward which science is heading.

In Kuhn's posthistoricist framework, all practices like science are heavily dependent upon historical and social factors. The vision of the scientist is molded *a priori* to his commitment to a paradigm, which represents his background, the basis of his communication with the scientific community that surrounds him, and, not least, the presupposition of the legitimacy of the results he reaches.

Even in science, like every other branch of knowledge, it is impossible to speak in absolute terms—to assume a universal and totalizing metahistorical vocabulary, in the light of which to judge the truth value of individual theories. The vision of scientific progress as a unidirectional process is rendered obsolete.

This radical refutation of a correspondence between theory and reality has brought down on Kuhn a storm of accusations, ranging from relativism to sociologism, and even to irrationalism, because of the thesis of the incommensurability of paradigms. Denying that the primary interest of science is to discover the truth in the absolute sense, and maintaining instead that its ray of possibility is limited to a specific historical range, Kuhn has been suspected of wanting to found science on less than purely rational bases, governed by the contingency of social instances and placed beyond any rigorous control. He has replied to this argument by trying to clarify the multidimensionality of the notion of paradigms in the 1974 essay "Second Thoughts on Paradigms," and he has, in any case, continued his explorations of the moments of historical discontinuity, as in his book *Black Body Theory and Quantum Discontinuity, 1894–1912*, published in 1979.

*

Since *The Structure of Scientific Revolutions* was published in 1962, your position has often been interpreted as a "cultural history" of scientific thought, rather than a theoretical speculation on science. Do you consider yourself a historian or a philosopher of science?

To be able to answer your question I must briefly reconstruct my itinerary, which looks quite unpredictable from today's point of view. I want to stress that I began my life as a physicist. I went through graduate school, but by the time I got my Ph.D. I became less and less sure that I wanted to be a physicist. I had never studied philosophy, and perhaps I would have studied more of it had it not been for World War II: I was an undergraduate at that time, and I clearly remember that there was a huge demand for people trained in physics and electronics, but very little indeed for philosophers.

There must have been a moment when you decided to make a break with experimental physics.

It happened by chance while I was working on my Ph.D. thesis in physics. I was asked by James Conant, then president of Harvard, whether I would like to be one of his two assistants in an experimental course in science for the nonscientists. This was a course in which he utilized case histories, historical examples of scientific advance. This was my first exposure to the history of science. I prepared a case, mostly on Galileo, and the transition from Aristotle to Newton, and I found it absolutely fascinating. Science looked very different from this historical perspective. It looked very different from the way it emerged from the texts of physics and philosophy I was used to reading.

At that time in the postwar period, what was the panorama of philosophy of science in America?

In this country, and at that time, it was not common at all for philosophers to utilize case histories. In fact, more than as a philosopher, I established myself as a historian of science, a field in which there was almost no professional training available in those days.

Can *The Structure of Scientific Revolutions* then be seen as the product of this initial phase of oscillation between history and the philosophy of science?

Yes, indeed, although it took me a long, long time to write it. I used examples taken from the history of science as well as from my experience as a scientist. I was always hoping to come back to the philosophical issues in it. The transition to philosophy is something in which I have been involved for years. *The Structure of Scientific Revolutions* is addressed to philosophical readers. But it is not fully about the philosophy of science. When I was writing it, I hoped that it would become an important book, but I never imagined that it would be read so widely, and, to tell the truth, also read so badly, by such a variety of readers. Today I would consider it part of a discipline that at that time did not even exist: the sociology of knowledge. The next step came when I decided I wanted to associate with philosophers, to work in a philosophy department. If I can get a few more ideas, I thought, I am going to try to identify myself and my work with the so-called professional community.

The notion of a "professional community," which is very similar to that of a "scientific community," brings me to the issue of your relationship with American tradition. Do you believe that your thought is in some way rooted in the American philosophical tradition? I mean the pragmatist line which, starting with Charles S. Peirce and William James, elaborated a connection between epistemological truth and the legitimation of a theory in the "research community."

As I said, I had had very little philosophy at that time. In *The Structure of Scientific Revolutions* I criticized the positivist tradition, but I hadn't read any Carnap. In fact, it was probably good for me, insofar as I had to deal only with the mature formulations. If I had followed all the professional elaborations, I would probably have written a very different book. On the other hand, I knew very little about pragmatism. I was aware that there was such a philosophical view, I had read a little William James, but it was the James of *The Varieties of Religious Experience* rather than *Pragmatism*. I had read some Dewey on pedagogical issues, but I have never been all that enthusiastic about pragmatism as a philosophical position. I would insist, for example, that some of the ways in which the notion of truth functions in the sciences are not strong enough to sustain a coherent theoretical definition, for instance, when truth doesn't get along with the law of noncontradiction. The notion of truth as the end of the road, as a limiting process or a justified and warranted belief, is not strong enough. This is one point on which I disagree with Hilary Putnam, with whom, on most other issues, I have a very positive dialogue.

I realize that it is a difficult question to answer, but if the notion of scientific community, which is so central to your theoretical elaboration on the concept of progress, does not derive from American pragmatism, where does it come from?

I don't particularly feel or think of myself as a participant or product of an American tradition, as against the general English-speaking one. The emphasis on communities, which is very important in *Structures,* although also very crude, was not at that time to be found in American philosophy. At least, not in any of the philosophy I had been exposed to. On the contrary, I was very much at the heart of the empiricist tradition.

Before getting to empiricism, I'd like to explore another area of thought that could be associated with your work, that is, the line of French epistemology from Gaston Bachelard to Michel Foucault. Throughout the twentieth century this line elaborates an apology for discontinuity. Truth—scientific truth for Bachelard and historical truth for Foucault—isn't the product or consequence of a linear process, but rather spills out from those *coupures*—fractures, cuts, differences—that represent the element of innovation and creativity in human development. Don't you think that a similar use of the notion of discontinuity can be found in your own work?

The French connection was important for me but it wasn't exactly in philosophy. It was Alexandre Koyré, and he was a historian. As a philosopher he didn't mean much to me. Philosophically, the most important figure was Emile Meyerson. It was he who first intro-

duced me to Karl Popper, whom I met at the time I gave the William
James Lectures at Harvard—that is, at the time of my transition
from history to philosophy. Popper suggested that I read Meyerson's
Identity and Reality, but, again, not for the philosophical side. I had
become somewhat more of an idealist as time had gone on. I didn't
like the philosophy, but I loved what it had led him to do with
historical examples. There was a post-Kantian tradition he was
bringing on—a way of looking at historical events that was transforming; and, although I don't feel at home with any Kantian under-
tone of philosophy, this specific aspect fascinated me.

**Karl Popper was very important in your evolution as a philoso-
pher. Could you say something more about your encounter with
him?**

I met him at the very end of the forties at the Harvard Society of
Fellows. He was not very happy with my James lectures, for he
pressed very strongly the notion that later theories embrace earlier
theories. I can remember him doing a diagram on the board in
which each new theory covered everything that an older theory
covered, and more besides. I was absolutely persuaded that you
could not do that, and that it was terribly important that you
couldn't. I interacted a bit, but not a great deal, with him at that
time: the most important product of that interaction for me was his
suggestion to read Meyerson. After that I saw him occasionally. He
came to Berkeley, from time to time, while Paul Feyerabend and I
were there.

**But your relationship with Popper was not always so cordial.
What were some of the issues over which your communication
became untenable?**

There was a whole series of them. I can't list them all, but a common
trait, for sure, is the notion of "logical falsifiability." I do not believe
in demarcation criteria. Sir Karl used to congratulate me upon having called attention to normal science, and then insisted that, of
course, one didn't really need it. Revolutions welcome revolutions.
"Science revolutionizes in perpetuity," he used to say. We were
so close that the way we came apart was not even visible to the
participants.

But do you feel, then, that you are closer to Popper or to that line of French epistemology which runs from Bachelard to Foucault?

While Koyré was important to my formation, there were also other non-Continental influences. As a matter of fact, I have gradually been fighting my way back from a generally empiricist orientation toward a more Continental position. In preparation for my first trip to Paris, I remember, I did read some Bachelard. But it was so close to my own thought that I did not feel I had to read lots and lots more. That is a terrible thing to have done. And I haven't read too much of Foucault either. *Les mots et les choses* is among the few. There is a way in which the French write on these matters that I find makes it very hard for me to read. Somebody who knew more about it than I once said to me: "What you have to do with this writing is simply to read it fast, don't think very much, and let it flow over you. Then see when you have stopped what it has done for you." But I cannot read that way.

That suggestion appears to have come from an empiricist rather than an expert on French philosophy.

In a sense it does. I have spent a good deal of time reading physics. It also has to do with the fact that when I read any sort of text, I read it trying to account for a word at a time. That's my way. It means looking for the things that don't work.

I'd like to concentrate awhile on Foucault, with whom your work has often been compared, particularly in Europe. At first glance, a visible connection could be established between your idea of science as a sequence of paradigms, evolving through revolutionary moments of rupture, and Foucault's archeological reconstruction of knowledge in its relation to the structures of power. Both visions of science and knowledge, yours and Foucault's, see discontinuity as a crucial moment in historical progress. Nevertheless, I have always felt a deep difference between you. Whereas Foucault thinks of discontinuity mainly in terms of its innovative value for the future, you consider scientific revolutions mainly in terms of their disruptive potential for the past.

I say that we must learn to see development and progress in science as something which is not drawn by a goal, as the way things really are at the far end, but as simple evolution from a starting point, like biological evolutions. Therefore I am very much sympathetic to Foucault's notion of *epistemes*, though I was quite uncertain they were as all-embracing as they appeared to be in his version. In the early parts of *Les mots et les choses* he discovers that words are used differently, and that you misread them simply going back in time. On the other hand, what I found objectionable about, and what I found destructive in Foucault was the account of the way one went from one *episteme* to another. The developmental process, the evolutionary process, all has to be part of a story that emphasizes *epistemes* and *coupures*. On the contrary, Foucault states that epistemological fractures can be represented but not explained, for they embody the "other" in itself. The interpretation of this otherness constituted Foucault's political involvement, which I never had. For Foucault it was less essential to talk about how one goes from one place to another, than to talk about where to go.

Aren't you thereby restoring centrality to the biological model in a sort of organicist fashion?

If the process is driven from behind, you then have to say what the response is, what direction it moves in as a result of a drive from behind. But if you believe, like Foucault, that history is being pulled from in front, you don't have to understand the process, changes become more trivial. . .

You were one of the first philosophers, especially in the scientific field, to deal with the question of incommensurability—a key concept especially in relation to the whole issue of the "other."

The notion of incommensurability has become increasingly important for me. And my own current work is more closely identifiable as an attempt to explain what incommensurability is and how such a thing could exist, than to explain any other single problem. Now I would put exclusive emphasis upon the linguistic component of it. I talk increasingly of incommensurability as untranslatability.

Intuitively, the connection is clear, but could you give an example?

The words that I am saying now are untranslatable, even though translations of them exist. There are places where you just can't make sense out of another language, and you have to learn that part of the language can't be translated. You have to learn the part of the language that is being used in the text, and then teach it to people and talk that language to them. You have to change the conceptual basis. So when I talk about Aristotle on the subjects of Motion and Matter and the Void, these are all words that exist in contemporary language, but they don't mean the same things. I have then to teach the old usage and the interconnections between them, and then, with those words in place, utilize them to explain what Aristotle is doing. I now increasingly emphasize the distinction between learning a new language or learning some parts of an ordered language, and translating from that language into the one you spoke before. It is often possible to learn languages that you cannot fully translate into your own.

You are proposing knowledge as a sort of capacity to contextualize each single scientific vocabulary within a specific cultural frame. But in what language are you stating this? I mean, is there a lingua franca into which you are in fact translating all specific vocabularies? Could it be history? and, if this were so, would you accept being considered a neo-historicist?

Let's take a very narrow notion of translation, for example the notion originally formulated by W. V. Quine, in which translation appears as a sort of mechanical process, governed by a manual that enables you to make substitutions from a given string of words in one language to a given string of words in another language. This is a form of translation that can't be done, I think, in a number of cases. You can do it with large parts of the text, but you can't do it with the whole. This is going to be my answer to the question of historicism, just as one says that poetry cannot be translated. There are nuances and associations on which many aspects of the poem may depend, that have to be caught in another language where the associations are different.

But science and poetry have different statutes of truth.

To the extent that scientific generalizations depend by their nature on preserving the precision, if you have a universal generalization that translates into something done only 80 percent of the time you must somehow have lost the science along the way—just as one loses the poetry when a poem is translated into something that preserves the literal meaning but not the associative meaning. If we rely on simply utilizing an unaltered modern vocabulary, we are not going to understand scientific texts of the past. There will be missing parts. The sort of history that used to be produced out of these texts is the one that read the texts that way and talked about what people did and didn't know. And this is also part of what makes science appear cumulative. You read a text of the past as aiming for what you already know, what you have been taught, and then sort it out into the things people in the past knew. And all this is facilitated by utilizing modern concepts, and trying to read them as approximations.

To what type of history are you inclined: perhaps to a multiplicity of local histories, not necessarily connected?

I don't want to think of history as itself a language. History is written "in a language," and sometimes the very best sorts of history are those that begin by setting the stage, showing what people believed, and seeking to persuade us that their beliefs were plausible. And then you move forward over time, and watch the language, and part of what you do is watch the language change.

But if you can never fully understand an old paradigm, if you don't have a lingua franca (history, rationality, truth) in which all specific vocabularies can be translated, how can you fully understand a new paradigm? In other words, the question of untranslatability applies not only to the past, but to communication among different theories in the present. It is not only a historical problem, but one of sociology and culture. How is it possible to legitimize a new truth if it does not possess a level of unitary verification on which to confront the truth values proposed by individual theories?

I don't say you cannot understand the past if you reformulate its content in the modern vocabulary. But you can't understand it without first learning the language in which it is formulated, which may be simply an older version of the English scientific vocabulary. Indeed, I think you can understand the past to the extent that you deal with it by recapturing the terms in which it was written. In *The Structure of Scientific Revolutions* I moved too easily from the experience of the historian looking back and trying to understand the text to the experience of the scientist moving forward. I spoke as though the same process was simply reversed in direction, and that's wrong, because it skips over the great deal of intervening material that is indispensable to reaching the old text. There may have been a whole lot of *coupures* along the way. But in a general way, if you look at the earliest versions of a new theory, the Copernican or the Einsteinian theory, they are always caught between using words partly in old ways and partly in new ones.

How do you see the difference between the perspective of the historian and the scientist today?

I think that steps forward are made in part by metaphor: what was initially metaphorical later becomes literal. You get a period of intervening communication in which one person is talking the old literal language and the other person is talking the new literal language, but they are communicating partially by virtue of metaphors. This is a period of misunderstanding, when communication is incomplete but not impossible. This is the time of experimental verification. You persuade people to come to your laboratory and look at what you're doing and talk about it. That's one of the ways in which language itself gets learned.

Do you think that the identification of this whole issue of the untranslatability of scientific vocabularies will have a practical influence on the future evolution of science?

Let us say *language learning* instead of translation. I will explain with an example. There is a certain group of connected terms that seem to occur together in closely related ways within the troublesome areas—the areas that do not quite make sense. After zillions of tries, one finally sees that if you "use" these words that you are not accustomed to use, suddenly you can see what these passages in the text mean. Nevertheless, you cannot put those meanings into your own modern language: you have to utilize what you have discovered, and teach other people to use the words in that way. That's why I say that the process of understanding involves language *learning* and cannot be reduced to *translation*, even after you have learned the other language. You still cannot go back and forth between the two. You cannot simply incorporate terms from another language into your own language and use them almost interchangeably with your own terms. If you want to speak in an Aristotelian vocabulary, fine. But you can't then, in the same or a neighboring sentence, use the same words in their subsequent Newtonian sense.

How is it possible to build a methodology of language learning, if you don't acknowledge the universality of a common *langue*?

There are very large common areas that you have to look for, but there are no rules saying in advance what those common areas must be. Usually the areas you can be surest of are those involving everyday observations. But that doesn't mean that you can even be sure that the words will go across there. It's simply the place where you can discover, by the attempt to read or to converse, which terms work and which terms do not work. Terms for emotions, terms for higher levels of scientific theory, and so forth, are very unlikely to work, to transfer back and forth, and they cannot be reduced to definitions in terms of the more elementary vocabulary. One has to discover them by attempting to participate in a dialogue with the text, or with the group that talks.

In a sense, you're saying that it is the scientific community that legitimizes the success or the failure of a translation, or the process of language learning. However, in centering on this notion of community, are we not back to the American pragmatist tradition?

Learning doesn't mean to translate from another language into your own, but rather to use a new language. Learning means learning to be native in the other language, even when you cannot translate it.

If it is better to refer to the processes of language learning rather than translation, what happens to the notion of untranslatability?

It isn't that one can't do a translation which is approximate. But at the level of approximation, the generalizations that you are translating are useless for scientific purposes. It is only when you conceive the sense in which they were once precise that they should emerge as precise generalizations. Here is where I see the parallel to literature, in particular poetry and drama, which depend on aspects of the words that go beyond their referential aspect.

It seems to me that you extend this linguistic approach to the entire scientific practice. Then, what kind of referentiality do you grant to language? If the whole universe, in its physical and historical sense, becomes part of an immanent linguistic system, what is left, as the deconstructionists say, "outside the text?"

I certainly believe in the referentiality of language. There is always something about referential matching involved in experience that tells you whether it is used to make true or false statements. There is a sense, a deep sense, in which I absolutely believe in the correspondence theory of truth. On the other hand, I also believe it's a trivial sort of correspondence. In the *Structure of Scientific Revolutions* I talked about word changing and changes of paradigm, and although I would like to put it in a more sophisticated way, basically I still believe in it.

From this point of view, how would you trace the evolution of your work?

I would define it as an increasing emphasis on language, which more and more plays the role that in *Structures of Scientific Revolutions* is played by the Gestalt changes. In that first book, there is quite a lot said about meaning changing. Now I talk more about referring terms, providing each one with a taxonomy. And even the change that has to do with incommensurability, I increasingly interpret as a taxonomic change. It is taxonomies that are commensurable with one another, the things one can really talk about.

What do you mean by a taxonomy? At what level are the taxonomies commensurable?

It's a complex and interrelated way of categorizing, partly innate, partly learned, that constitutes the taxonomic aspects of language.

Could taxonomy be considered a synonym for scientific paradigm, which, starting with your first book, is how you defined the various systems of scientific knowledge throughout history?

I'm not sure I would use the term paradigm in such a wide sense anymore.

How does your paradigmatic theory affect the ethical responsibility of science?

If I had to rewrite the *Structure of Scientific Revolutions,* a notion I would emphasize much more is the one of puzzle solving. Scientists are trained to solve puzzles, and there is a considerable ideology involved in all that. There have to be more and more puzzles, more and more precise solutions to older puzzles. So there is a goal. It's just not a goal at the more metaphysical level. It's not a question of getting closer and closer to what nature is like, but it is a current of challenge to the scientist of any given generation. The enterprise still has a goal. It's not out there, it's right here.

You mean that the objective of science is precisely the negation of limit. Aren't limits immanent to scientific practice itself?

To give an example, you're getting closer and closer to how things are really like. How are you going to set limits to that? The problem is just as vexing as when you say, "Look, there are some things mankind would be better off if we did not know." But then, of course, the scientists would say, "The truth will not hurt." The situation doesn't feel any different to me with respect to those important moral and social issues. I don't want to say that they lie outside the philosophy of science, but they are not problems to which I feel myself making any particular contribution. Popper once said that there is one thing that was unpredictable, that nobody could have ever predicted: the invention of the wheel. You cannot predict the next scientific discovery.

INDEX